YOUTH MINISTRY
POST-CHRISTIAN WORLD

A HOPEFUL WAKE-UP CALL

FOREWORD BY CHAP CLARK

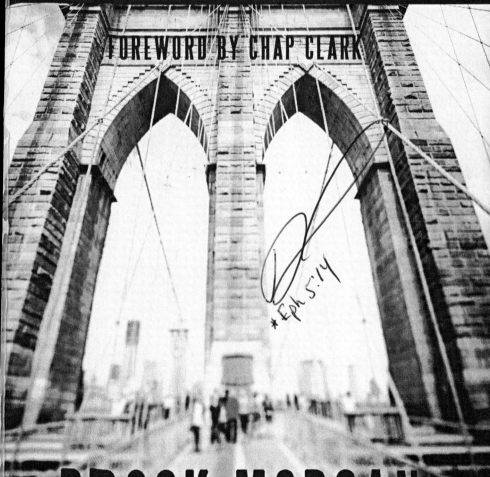

BROCK MORGAN

ENDORSEMENTS

I really, really hope—enthusiastically hope—that youth workers all over the country will read Brock Morgan's book *Youth Ministry in a Post-Christian World*. Please don't get hung up over the phrase post-Christian. Whether you're afraid of that phrase or think you are fully informed on the subject, this book is for all youth workers who want to do thoughtful, transformational and theologically sound youth ministry. I think and reflect a lot about culturally relevant, theologically robust youth ministry, but this book challenged me to examine my own youth ministry praxis and commitment. I'm rarely impressed with youth ministry books but this one is so passionately on target that I will sing it's praises for a long time to come.
Mike King
President/CEO, Youthfront; Author of *Presence Centered Youth Ministry*

After reading the draft manuscript, I contacted the folks at The Youth Cartel and pre-ordered 25 copies! No joke. Brock's insight into post-Christian culture and ministry to teens within such a culture are inspiring and refreshing. His optimism for the future burns brightly which makes for a helpful resource that not only deconstructs the current reality but also faithfully constructs a new way forward. This book will undoubtedly assist any youth worker in their pursuit of guiding teens into spiritual formation for the mission of God in a post-Christian culture.
Chris Folmsbee
Author of *A New Kind of Youth Ministry* and Pastor of Group Life Ministry at Church of the Resurrection, Leawood, KS

Whatever your church traditions and views of postmodern Christian relativism might be, this book is important for every youth pastor, leader, or mentor. Brock's 20-plus years of in-the-trenches youth ministry, combined with his discerning eye towards society, culture, and faith, lead to reflections that are insightful, truthful, and challenging, and then to responses that are theologically grounded, practicably sound, and eminently hopeful.
Crystal Kirgiss
Literature Professor at Purdue University and author of many books including *More Than Skin Deep*

Youth Ministry in a Post-Christian World is, above all, a story of honesty and hope. There's not a youth worker alive who won't resonate with Brock Morgan's unassuming self-portrait of a ministry (and a youth minister) coming to terms with America's first explicitly "post-Christian" decades. I felt like I knew the youth in these pages; I groaned with recognition at Morgan's failures and smiled at God's grace-giving surprises. Above all, Morgan gives teenagers—and those who love them—what we are desperate for: permission to trust in a God who is far bigger than the moment before us. If you're looking for another program manual of youth ministry how-to's and free advice, keep looking. But if you need a friend in the trenches, whose journey will make you feel a little less alone, then this is your next read.

Kenda Creasy Dean
Professor of Youth, Church and Culture,
Princeton Theological Seminary
Author of *Almost Christian* and *Practicing Passion*

What you're going to hear in this book is the passionate heart of a thoughtful youth worker who is unwilling to let standard youth ministry operating procedure get in the away of authentic, vital ministry. You won't have to agree with everything Brock says to recognize that he's asking important questions. This isn't just hand-wringing. Particularly in the last few chapters there are some helpful, practical steps for the way forward. Well-worth a read!

Dr. Duffy Robbins
Professor of Youth Ministry, Eastern University, St. Davids, PA

Brock Morgan is a real-life youth pastor who, like a fine wine, has aged well. Whether you're a youth ministry veteran or just stepping onto the scene, this book is worth reading, simply for one reason—it's honest. We need more thoughtful transparency in our youth ministry conversing and self-reflecting. Brock shows us a way.

Steven Argue
Life Development Director at Mars Hill Church in Grand Rapids, Michigan

Last year, I returned to our city's public schools. Honestly, I'm not sure why I stopped going to them so often. It was a gradual shift and eventually the schools were off my radar completely. When I returned, I realized what I had been missing, that programs had taken precedence over people, and what I desperately needed as a human being if I was going to continue to loving and creating safe spaces for teenagers in our church to receive and experience grace. Brock, in his new book, takes us on a similar journey that shows us where we've been and where we could be heading if we don't engage the heart of Christ, first in our own lives, and then in the development of our ministry plans. We need this book!
Brooklyn Lindsey
Authored of *A Parent's Guide to Understanding Teenage Girls and Confessions of a Not-So-Supermodel*, youth pastor at Highland Park Church of the Nazarene.

Brock Morgan is one of the most adaptable youth workers I know. He's genuine in his love for God and courageous in his love for people. Brock is an innovator, but not in the popular sense, where an unstable visionary cooks up new ways of doing ministry in the name of being a catalyst or change agent. Brock innovates because he loves people, he's observant and he's genuinely expects that the ministry he leads will be effective. This makes for unique stories and unique youth ministry that can't be replicated. Youth Ministry in a Post-Christian World is a glimpse into the heart of a great leader and the heart that makes Brock so good at what he does. It's not blueprint for your youth ministry, however, the best youth pastors will read his stories and learn to be more themselves. Maybe a few will even have the courage to innovate from love, observation and hope that Brock as he leads his church to minister in a post-Christian world.
Mark Riddle
Founder/Principal of The Riddle Group

This book is really needed and worth your investment of time if you work with students, especially if you work with teens in a church setting. Here are three reasons why: First, Brock is a practitioner. He has and does live in the world of teenagers. And he does this in the context of a local church. He knows all the opportunities, challenges and realities of doing ministry in a local congregation. It is a filter that serves him well as he continually ties his concepts and insights into practical implications and direction that you will find useful. Second, Brock is a truth teller. In this book he continually tells us how things are not how we pretend they are or wish they were. "You shall know the truth and the truth shall set you free,"… to do real ministry in a new reality. Brock sheds light on our students, our culture, our churches and our approach to reaching this generation. And finally, Brock shares hope. This is not a dissertation of death, far from it. This book is an invitation to reaching kids and calling them into an amazing life with Jesus. Yes, Brock does all the heavy lifting and critical thinking to make sure this is a thoughtfully and theologically sound response to the world we find our ministries in. In the end you will find yourself better equipped and excited to engage with students.

Tic Long
Executive Pastor of Journey Community Church, La Mesa, CA, and former Executive Director of Youth Specialties

Youth Ministry in a Post-Christian World

Publisher: Mark Oestreicher
Managing Editor: Anne Marie Miller
Editor: Laura Gross
Design: Adam McLane
Creative Director: George Jetson (and Jane, his wife)

ISBN-13: 0988741385
ISBN-10: 978-0-9887413-8-6

The Youth Cartel, LLC
www.theyouthcartel.com
Email: info@theyouthcartel.com

Born in San Diego
Printed in the U.S.A.

Contents

FOREWORD

I still consider myself a youthworker. (That's right—one word, not two. Old school!) However, as God has led, it's getting harder for me to say that in a way that people can understand. I am now not only a professor (of youth, family and culture—the academic basis for youth ministry in my world), but a *seminary* professor (to many, just one more step removed from the action). But even worse, I am an *associate provost*. (Okay, I'm an associate provost who still teaches a bunch, but it's still a giant leap removed from professor!)

I may no longer work day to day with kids, or sit in meetings where I am ignored but still have to be there, or try to convince people who are decades older than I am that I understand their kids and am committed to them as a family. But after four decades of working in and around the youth ministry world, it's still in my bones . . . it's a part of my DNA. I still build these odd but solid relationships with kids, where appropriate. I still speak to and, I believe, connect with them. And I actively listen to and study teenagers and young (some would say "emerging") adults. So, yep, I'm still in the youth ministry game.

That said, there are some good and some not-so-good aspects of being one of those "I am a youthworker, but I speak, write, and teach for a living" type of youthworkers. It's not that I'm out of touch, because I feel like I'm as in tune with what it means to come alongside a teenager as ever. But so much has changed since the days when I gave up Friday nights for high school football and basketball games, and when a week at camp was considered the family vacation. It's not up for debate that so much has changed in the last 40 years. The only questions are "To what extent?" and "At what cost?" This is true for parents, for educators, and even for coaches; but it's especially true when it comes to youth ministry.

That's why I'm so grateful for Brock Morgan and the hundreds—if not thousands—of folks out there who have not only continued serving in youth ministry day to day, but have done it well. And I am grateful for this book.

For a brief time I was Brock's boss at Glendale Presbyterian Church in Glendale, California. But we got to know each other pretty well during that period. He'd been around as a "professional" for quite a while even then. Brock was a committed and gifted middle school director, and his wife Kelsey was just as gifted and equally engaged in loving and nurturing sixth, seventh, and eighth graders for the kingdom. As often happens, our church paid for one and got two. And like almost every ministry I've seen in those cases, they took every advantage.

I've followed Brock and Kelsey's ministry efforts ever since. I've heard him speak. I've read what he's written. I've been around him as a family man. And I've spent time with him among those he is called to lead. I'm glad Brock took on this writing project. And there are five reasons why I believe he is the right guy at the right time to write *Youth Ministry in a Post-Christian World*.

First, of all the people who started their full-time youth ministry careers in the late 1980s and early 1990s, there aren't many who've consistently stuck with it ever since. Brock has not only proven faithful to his calling (which is number four), but he's lived and operated through one of the biggest, if not *thee* biggest, shifts affecting ministry to adolescents since we first started viewing teenagers as a defined population. Brock was trained in how to do great '80s youth ministry, and he excelled at it during the '90s. As the culture changed, as systems changed, and as the kids themselves changed, the church, for the most part, has not changed its approach to youth ministry. Brock was caught up in the turmoil of that transition, and he not only survived, but also thrived. It takes a special person to endure the challenges of living through one season of ministry with all of its expectations and demands, and then commit to *unlearning* and recalibrating everything that "worked" in the past. Brock is one of those special people.

Second, Brock has held on to what's most important. Amidst all of the changes, two things remain constant in his approach to youth ministry: God is worthy of our praise, gratitude, and very lives; and people—children, teens, and adults—need to know they are worthy of respect and care. In the '80s and '90s, a good youthworker could get hundreds of enthusiasts to commit to the program. A *great* youthworker would know that while numbers might indicate a healthy ministry, what really mattered was the compassionate lordship of Jesus Christ and a love for people. In the 2000s and beyond, a good youthworker could keep the basic programmatic ship moving forward for at least a season, and perhaps even foster enough observable "depth" and "growth" that he or she was able to remain employed. Today, a *great* youthworker realizes that while programs are sometimes helpful, they ultimately don't matter the way they used to. People and relationships and mission are what the church is called to. In the '90s, Brock was a great youthworker. Today, Brock is a great youthworker.

Third, Brock is directly in touch with how the changing culture impacts relationships with and ministry to adolescents. He goes right to the heart of social media's presence and influence, helping us see that when kids compare themselves to others, they now have *measurables* such as the number of "friends" and "likes," causing a deeper sense of relational competition that constantly lurks just beneath the surface. His stories about kids and families are fresh and real.

Fourth, while Brock doesn't pretend to have simple answers to complex and fluid questions, he at least dives in with his take on what the youthworker's role is today. You might not agree with everything he presents (I'm not even sure I agree with everything he says!) but he does get us thinking. I especially appreciated his notion of a "Starbucks spirituality" and his story about the girl in his youth group who proudly shared that she'd become a Buddhist. Brock isn't interested in a sanitized version of "doing" youth ministry. Instead, after all of Brock's years of experience and training, he's willing to sit down with the reader and ask, "Is this what you've seen? What about this?" I, for one, find this refreshing.

Finally, I appreciate Brock's willingness to take us on a journey to new and, at times, uncharted territory. Kids have changed, their developmental abilities and realities have changed, and there are many times when we find ourselves at a loss when it comes to leading and loving kids for the sake of Christ. Yet, Brock's desire to stay in there and slug it out, to ask the hard questions—of himself and even the "sages" he praises—is what all of us need.

I heard Brené Brown speak last week, and she loves to quote Teddy Roosevelt. I thought of Brock when she shared this quote:

> *"It is not the critic who counts; not the man who points out how the strong man stumbles, or where the doer of deeds could have done them better. The credit belongs to the man who is actually in the arena . . . "*

In summary, Brock lives what he writes, and the following passage from his book demonstrates why I am a fan of Brock Morgan:

> *"The essence of youth ministry is to create environments where students can experience the warmth of God. With every talk we give, every game or activity we lead, and every time we run into students at the mall, they experience God's warmth. And that's because our relationship with Jesus is our ministry."*

Chap Clark
Author, *Hurt 2.0*
Professor of Youth, Family and Culture
Fuller Theological Seminary
Gig Harbor, WA

ACKNOWLEDGEMENTS

I want to begin by thanking a few people who've helped shape me and have become, as Paul writes in Philippians 2, my "deep-spirited friends." I owe them a very pleasant debt of gratitude.

First, I want to thank Kelsey, my amazing wife, friend, and ministry partner. I love you more than I can express, and I am so grateful for the journey we've been on these past 22 years. You have set the pace in so many ways. Thank you for continuing to run after kids with me, and for the detailed way you show me love every day. Thank you for reading and rereading and editing so much of this book. I LOVE you so much!

Dancin—I am so honored to be your daddy! You are spectacular, and I love everything about you. Thank you, sweetie, for how open and caring and loving you are to every person around you.

I want to thank my church, Trinity Church in Greenwich, Connecticut, for giving me the time to write this book and for the partnership we share in being salt and light in our community. This book grew out of our life together. I especially want to thank Drew Williams for his amazing leadership and wise counsel at several junctures. I love how even when you confront me, it doesn't feel so bad because of your beautiful British accent.

Dean and Susan Allen—thank you for generously allowing me to use your homes to write. You guys are just so generous and help set the tone in our community. I'm grateful!

The youth team at Trinity—Ben, Jen, Hanna, and all of you who are in the trenches with us—thank you for your heart and vision in reaching and loving students who are growing up in this complex post-Christian world. You all just blow me away!

My parents, Paul and Carol—I couldn't have had better parents. I love being your son!

My sisters, Sasha and Vangela—you are beauty to the core.

Dr. Bill Brown—thank you for your investment in me. Your mentorship has meant more to me than I can express.

Tim Galleher—you set me on a path and showed me how to truly bless a community.

Mark Helsel—10 years ago you began dreaming with me about what the future of youth ministry might be and how we could continue to evolve as youth workers in this ever-changing landscape of youth culture. Thank you.

Tic Long and the former and current YS teams—thank you for believing in me. I am full of gratitude for how you took a big chance on me. I still remember with such fondness how Tic asked me to come to work at Youth Specialties.
YS One Day crew—I miss those days! Chap, I appreciate your profound influence over me both up close and from a distance.

Duffy, your prayers for me were coveted, and God blessed me through you.

Marko, Adam, and The Youth Cartel family—thank you for being sounding boards, feedback givers, and, mostly, lifelong friends. I'm blown away by how generous you've been to me. Marko, thank you for hanging in there with me and for the favor you've shown me. I don't deserve even half of what you've given to me. The next cigar is on me!

Brock Morgan

INTRODUCTION

MIGHT AS WELL START AT THE BEGINNING

I remember the moment like it was yesterday. In fact every time I think about it, I cringe a little. At the time, I was the brand-new youth pastor at the church, and my youth group was full of doubters and skeptics. I wanted to prove them all wrong. So I worked all week on a talk that I believed would change everything. Because, you know, talks do that. But I was convinced this talk would open the students' minds and illuminate how wrong they really were. I would show them that if they truly used their brains, they'd come to the same conclusions I had.

What's funny is that I was so convinced that once they heard my brilliant speech, they'd all repent and come running down to the altar to receive Jesus as their Lord and Savior. *What a perfect time to do communion!* I thought. You can see where this is going, huh?

After I finished delivering my "brilliant" message, I explained the bread and the cup. And then I invited the students to come forward and receive communion. No one moved. Now put yourself in this scenario for a moment: You speak passionately about why faith makes sense, you explain the elements of the communion, and then you invite your students to come forward to receive it . . . and no one blinks, no one prayerfully considers it, no one moves. No one gets up to participate in communion. No one responds. *Not one person.*

Awkward!

Obviously, I needed a new strategy.

I've been a youth worker for over 23 years now, and most of those years have been spent in Southern California during the heyday of American youth ministry. Back then we'd build an awesome youth room and play cool Christian music videos on big screens, and tons of kids would come to youth group. We'd organize area youth rallies and see 2,000 high schoolers show up to eat free pizza and play Nintendo 64 on the big screen. I'd preach the gospel to hundreds of students on a Wednesday night, and a majority of them would invite Christ into their lives.

But as the years have gone by, I've noticed a few things. Kids look at me differently. Their questions have changed—they are deeper, more personal, and usually loaded. The answers I gave students 15 years ago will no longer suffice. To be honest, those answers don't even work for *me* anymore.

The world is changing and it's changing us—in some ways for the better. It requires us to reconsider the ways we think about and interact with the people around us. The good news is that thoughtful, humble, and curious Christians are making headway in today's world. However, many of us remain stuck in the old systems and structures, using methods that were brilliantly effective at one time. But our culture has changed.

And if we're honest, we'll admit that the things that once worked so well are no longer cutting it with our students.

My prayer is that this book will cause youth workers to lift their heads, that it will stretch them and even shake them up a bit. But please know that I write this as a practitioner. I am not a youth ministry professor at a seminary; I'm a youth worker too. In fact, as I write this introduction, I'm also thinking about the game I'm leading tonight with our middle schoolers. It has something to do with balloons and shaving cream . . . but I digress.

What I've discovered over the past 10 years is that I have to let go of the junk I've accumulated throughout my entire life of youth ministry—the methods and the mindsets that have boxed Jesus in and kept students out. As you read this little book, I hope you'll allow the systems and structures of your own ministry to be challenged and take an honest look at your students, the church, the world, and yourself. Hopefully we'll emerge from this exercise better equipped to represent and extend the reign of Jesus in a world that, at best, isn't interested.

Please note: This book contains the story of what I've stumbled onto in my youth ministry work. It's the story of how an evangelical modern Christian has tried to make a difference in the lives of pluralistic, post-modern students. It's the story about repeatedly going back to the drawing board and trying desperately to hear the cutting-edge voice of Jesus. My prayer is that you will join me on this humbling and scary, yet wonderful journey.

CHAPTER ONE

WHAT IS THE WORLD COMING TO?!

The first time I heard about post-Christianity was when a fellow youth worker told me something he'd overheard. He said a friend of his asked a young pregnant woman if she and her husband had thought of any names for their baby. She answered with this little bomb: "We really haven't thought of a name yet, but one thing we *do* know is that it won't be a biblical name." This took him aback, so he asked her why. She responded matter-of-factly, "Oh, because we live in a post-Christian world."

When I first heard this story, that term kind of troubled me. "post-Christian world" sounded apocalyptic, like something from Mel Gibson's *Mad Max* film from 1979. Was I going to have to wear a sleeveless leather jacket and swimming goggles while driving my hopped-up VW Beetle through the desert wasteland? It sounded like the end of the world—especially the way people were talking about it. In describing the future, they said things like, "There will be no moral compass, and within 50 years the faith will be lost. The world will be like Sodom and Gomorrah." It was quite the dramatic sentiment, and it caused youth workers and parents alike to purchase lots of books about the future doom.

As a young youth worker, I attended the National Youth Workers Convention and heard a speaker tell us to look to Europe. He said we were about 20 years behind them; so if we wanted to know where America was headed, we needed to look that way. Then the speaker described a world that a young and forward-thinking youth guy like myself couldn't even fully grasp. It wasn't doomsday or end-of-the-world type stuff; it was just something I couldn't instantly apply. I was working in the trenches with American teenagers in Southern California, and they weren't post-Christian at all. So I went back to work with my students and did the best I could.

But as the years went on, from time to time I'd notice things. Like how the Christian faith wasn't having as much of an impact on students' thinking. The biblical stories were either lost on them or, more importantly, just didn't matter to this new generation. And so as any thoughtful youth worker would do, I started researching how I might stay effective in my ministry to students. You see, when what you've always done has worked just fine, why should you change anything?

However, if you happen to notice that what you've always done is no longer sticking or completely resonating with your students, then this realization should cause you to go back to the drawing board. And it will keep you humble. I felt like I was living on a different planet than my kids. I was standing in the old modern world, and my kids were living in a world where the Christian story no longer mattered. Oh sure, I had a cool goatee and dressed like a member of Pearl Jam, but I was no longer traveling the same road as my students.

It wasn't that I suddenly noticed these teenagers were horny or they wanted to party and get drunk. Students have always wanted to do those things (I still do.) But their mentality was changing. We youth leaders weren't as effective, the gospel wasn't making as much sense to them, and culturally the faith was no longer having an impact in centering our community. Before I knew it, I was working with post-Christian students.

Stuart Murray defines post-Christianity (or "post-Christendom") as "The culture that emerges as the Christian faith loses coherence within a society that has been definitively shaped by the Christian story and as the institutions that have been developed to express Christian convictions decline in influence."[1]

The Christian faith losing coherence? Check.

Christian institutions declining in influence? Check.

It's a difficult shift to perceive when all the people you hang out with think just like you do. But if you get outside the bubble and really listen, you'll discover that things really have changed in the world, and they continue to change. You see, a post-Christian world is one in which Christianity is no longer the dominant religion or even the dominant mindset. An evolution has occurred over the past 50-plus years. Slowly and gradually over time, our society has begun to assume values, cultures, and worldviews that aren't Judeo-Christian. At that youth workers' conference 20 years ago, I was told this was going to happen. But I didn't listen. And now that time is upon us.

America is in the midst of this transition from a Judeo-Christian value system into a post-Christian mindset. Oh, you can bet the church is doing a lot of kicking and screaming right now. That's what happens when the top dog is no longer the top dog. It's called a power struggle. And when something that's been dominant within a culture starts to lose its voice, power, and influence . . . well, it can get pretty ugly. Watch the news and you'll see that it's not just ugly; it's downright toxic.

Some of you might be thinking, *No way, Brock! You're wrong. I've read the stats and I've seen the research. The majority of people in America and around the world are Christians.*

To that I say, "Really? That's what you think?"

Most youth workers are very familiar with the work of Christian Smith. He's done the most extensive research on teenage spirituality in America called The National Study of Youth and Religion. What he and his colleagues found was that the most pervasive religious beliefs of teenagers is not Christianity, but what he calls Moralistic Therapeutic Deism (MTD):[2]

> Moralism = Be good.
> Therapeutic = Feel good.
> Deism = God is just in the background.

It's fairly obvious that the dangerous, radical, die to self, pick up your cross and follow Jesus kind of faith has lost steam in our culture. Our students aren't growing up in that world.

In the summer of 2010, I took a new job at Trinity Church in Greenwich, Connecticut, just north of New York City. People tend to move to Greenwich once they've "made it" in The Big Apple. It's a small city full of successful artists, actors, musicians, and Wall Street money people; it's also a melting pot of cultures, ideas, and worldviews. For the better part of the previous 23 years, I'd worked with students on the West Coast. So going to New England was a huge move for my family. And while post-Christianity is alive and well on the West Coast—especially in the Northwest—moving to Greenwich provided me with some visible evidence of what's happening in youth culture today.

When I arrived in this new town, word had already gotten out amongst the students in our church that I was really into Jesus. Initially, I took that as a compliment. But I soon realized, um, not so much . . . . See, the church had recently hired a lead pastor from England who was very "Jesus-y." And now the church had hired me, another "Jesus-y" bloke except worse—I was from California, and I have a couple tattoos.

Granted, the students' rebellion toward me was partly because of the transition. They of course loved their previous youth pastor, and I represented change, which teenagers don't like. But I also represented conservative Christianity, which is very offensive to them.

If you want to see post-Christianity in full swing in America, just look to New England where the church is either dying or dead. Beautiful old buildings stand empty in the center of towns. It reminds me of the old children's poem that says,

"Here is the church, and here is the steeple, open the doors, and where are all the people?" Well, the people are long gone. They left many years ago.

To keep their churches "alive," pastors and congregational leaders have become property managers, turning their buildings into rental facilities where music lessons, choirs, AA meetings, acting troops, and exercise classes can rent out space. But there is barely any Christian community life happening inside of those four walls. The post-Christian world is now in full force, and the church is not even a blip on the screen.

While I was speaking at an amazing youth camp in Michigan, I met the worship band that had been brought in for the weekend. When they learned that I'm a youth pastor in New England, they were amazed. They're from Canada, and they tour all over the United States. But they said when they get to New England, they just drive on home because there are no gigs in sight.

Now back to my initial arrival in Greenwich. Picture my wife and me sitting in a living room with about 20 students. I asked them, "So tell me, what do you guys love about the youth group?"

Here's where they drew the line in the sand for this "Jesus-y" youth worker. One student stood and spoke for the rest of them, saying, "What we love about our youth group is that no one preaches Jesus here, and we can believe whatever we want to believe."

Huh. Okay. After that, my wife and I got in our car and drove back to California, never to return. No, not really. We got in the car and sat quietly for a moment. Then I blurted out, "What in the hell have we gotten ourselves into?!"

In Greenwich, every public school student takes a class called "The Myth of Creation." It's not a science class about evolution; it's a class that basically breeds agnostic thinking. Our students have grown up surrounded by liberal reductionism, and the church has no voice in the community mindset. The biblical narrative no longer has any coherence, and its influence left the building not long after Elvis did.

I know this may not sound anything like youth ministry in Atlanta or other parts of the nation. But the world is flat, which means my students and your students are not so far apart. If you aren't seeing the post-Christian culture's impact upon your students yet, then it's just around the corner. I speak at youth camps all across the country, and I'm always blown away by how the kids ask the same types of questions and with that same look in their eyes. No matter where they're from, students are having the same kinds of thoughts. They all listen to the same music, watch the same movies, and are growing up in a world whose main religion is Moralistic Therapeutic Deism at best.

I took a World Religions class in high school. We learned about Buddhism, Islam, Hinduism, the folk religions, Judaism, as well as many others. Back then, the students in my class were either Christians or nothing at all. In fact, except one of my friend's parents who were nominal Buddhists, I didn't know anyone who believed differently than my family or I did. Today, this is not the case. Students are growing up with different worldviews and different religions all around them. As a kid it was easy for me to dismiss a religion, a philosophy, or even a perspective when I didn't know anyone who held those beliefs. But when the Buddhist is your best friend, when the liberal is your cousin, when the Muslim is on your basketball team, when the agnostic is your neighbor . . . well then, that changes everything.

Our students are growing up in a pluralistic society that's much different than the world in which you and I grew up. And if you're smack-dab in the midst of adolescence and your top goals are to fit in and not stand out, to be different by being just like everyone else, then the acceptance of all things is an important value to have. This is the world we're living in, and it's the collision of all things.

Al Mohler, president of Southern Seminary in Louisville, Kentucky, wrote:

In candor, we must admit that the Church has been displaced. Once an authoritative voice in the culture, the Church is often dismissed, and even more often ignored. At one time, the influence of the Church was sufficient to restrain cultural rebellion against God's moral commandments, but no longer. The dynamic of the culture-shift marches onward. . . . The worldview of most Americans is now thoroughly secularized, revolving around the self and its concerns, and based on relativism as an axiom. We Americans have become our own best friend, our own

therapist, our own priest, and our own lawgiver. The old
order is shattered, the new order is upon us.³

The Barna Group recently conducted research on religion
in America, and they specifically looked deeper into this
post-Christian trend. Based on a random survey of 42,855
people, they found that 37 percent of Americans are post-
Christian and that percentage is climbing. In addition, this 37
percent labeled themselves as either atheistic or agnostic, in
disagreement with the Bible, not committed to Jesus, and not
participating in a church.

Even more interesting were the differences they discovered
between generations:

> *The differences by generation are striking, and they suggest*
> *a less "Christianized" nation in the decades to come. The*
> *younger the generation, the increasingly post-Christian it*
> *is compared with its predecessors. Nearly half of Mosaics*
> *(48%) qualify as post-Christian compared with two-fifths*
> *of Busters (40%). One-third of Boomers (35%) and*
> *one-quarter of Seniors (28%) are post-Christian. These*
> *patterns are consistent with other studies that show the*
> *increasing percentage of "Nones" [i.e., adults who claim*
> *no religious affiliation] among younger generations.⁴*

What this data tells us is that post-Christianity is a booming
trend.

After I'd been at Trinity Church for a few months, the time
finally came to take the youth group on a weekend retreat. Up

until then, we'd seen very little openness to the gospel, but we just kept loving students, listening to them, and praying for a breakthrough. On Saturday night, the unimaginable happened. After I finished speaking, everyone worshipped—let me say that again, *everyone worshipped*—and God moved in an amazing way. Students all over that room were repenting of their rebellion, giving their lives to Jesus, and praying for each other. It was one of those nights that keeps you in youth ministry and makes you believe your investment is finally paying off.

Afterward I was sitting with a group of tenth grade guys, and they were all sharing what Jesus had done in their hearts. Honestly, I was floating on air. I couldn't believe what God was doing and what they were sharing. Yep, I was floating! But then a kid named John spoke up, and I came crashing back to earth.

He said, "Tonight, God told me that reincarnation is true." I looked at him and wondered if he was joking around, but I soon realized he was serious.

Thank goodness his buddy cut through the awkward silence and said, "Dude, wrong religion."

It's interesting to look back and see how our country got to where we are today. America began as the brave new world that welcomed all. Posted symbolically on the Statue of Liberty are the words *"Give me your tired, your poor, your huddled masses yearning to breathe free . . . "* So every tribe and tongue has been coming to America ever since. They accepted our invite. But what if those masses of people arrive with different religions and worldviews? And what if they bring their own cultures and start influencing American culture? What if they don't look like us? What if they don't think or act like us? What if white Christian America is no longer the majority? What if this so-called "Christian nation" eventually dies out and a new post-Christian world emerges? Well, people will start freakin' out. Those who were once in the majority begin using words like "us" and "them," and then the culture wars begin.

This is what's happening in our nation right now, currently, at this very minute—whether or not you admit it or see it. Post-Christianity is in full swing, and it's growing. Christendom is now dead, and we need to get over it. The bigger problem is the fact that the church saw this coming for a long time, but it didn't respond well. It all started happening during the nineteenth century when liberalism began its rise and Darwinism was gaining steam. Because of the church's poor response to Darwin's theories about evolution, science was now on the offense, and Christianity was left to play defense. Instead of embracing science, we defended our position and insulated ourselves against the world. We appeared angry, unintelligent, and backward to those on the outside. Instead of joining the conversation, we started preaching to the choir, turned inward, and lost our voice in the world. And now the church can't get over it.

At one time Christianity was known for its leaders in thinking, bringing justice to the world, and creatively engaging the culture around them. We started schools such as Princeton and organizations like the Red Cross, but then we replaced those things with the Christian Right. We turned against culture and taught our children how to defend their faith. Christians used to play offense, but then we became defensive specialists. And this change in our position created the "us versus them" construct. I don't blame Christians for responding the way they did. It was a scary time. I get it. But how we respond *now* is just as vital. We must take lessons from that time period and apply what we learn to how we respond today.

Last night I was talking on the phone with the father of one of the students in our ministry. He was brought up Catholic but rejected the faith when he was in high school. He is the typical post-Christian adult living in New England, but recently he came to faith and started attending our church. During our phone conversation, he told me he was very concerned that his son's grandparents were having a bad influence on him. Naturally I thought he was talking about his own parents who are agnostic.

I said, "Oh, don't worry. They won't turn your son into an agnostic; he has a very strong faith."

The father said, "I'm not talking about *my* parents. I'm talking about my *wife's* parents—they're evangelical Christians. I'm afraid they'll turn him into one of those!"

I laughed and said, "So you don't mind if he becomes agnostic; you just don't want him to become an evangelical?"

"Exactly!" he said.

What he sees as "evangelical Christianity" in America turns him off. Christians appear closed-minded and judgmental, and he doesn't want his son to become like that.

POST-CHRISTIANITY IS NOT GLOBAL

This post-Christian world isn't a world at all. If you look at global Christianity, you'll notice a few things. First, the church isn't dying; it's actually growing. Timothy C. Tennent's brilliant book *Invitation to World Missions* gives us an amazing perspective and insights into what's happening globally. Yes, Europe is in full swing within the post-Christian era, and America is just now entering into it. But there is a new face to global Christianity, and it's no longer Caucasian. It's Korean, African, Chinese, and Indian.

The church is booming in those locations because Christians have learned to live and minister in a culture that hasn't been sympathetic to their faith. They don't have a political machine talking for them; rather, Christians are creatively and humbly bringing the gospel and extending the beautiful reign of Jesus to those around them. Great writers and theologians are now coming out of these countries. And amazingly, they see America as a huge mission field, so they're sending mission-aries to us. We've become the region that must be reached.

Tennent writes:

> *Today there are over 367 million Christians in Africa, comprising one-fifth of the entire Christian church. Throughout the twentieth century a net average gain of 16,500 people were coming to Christ every day in Africa.*

From 1970 to 1985, for example, the church in Africa grew by over six million people. During that same time . . . 4,300 people per day were leaving the church in Europe and North America.[5]

There is amazing growth happening in South Korea as well, with over 20 million Christians living there. This number is pretty significant considering there are only 49 million people in the entire country. In America that percentage (41%) may not seem so massive when you consider our nation's history with a large majority of Americans claiming to be Christian. Just remember that these countries are and have been pre-Christian for thousands of years.

A church in America is considered to be a megachurch if at least 2,000 people attend its services. And some of America's largest churches have as many as 30,000 members. By contrast, Tennent writes that "South Korea is widely regarded as the home of the modern church growth movement, which is exemplified by . . . the Yoido Full Gospel Church." It's the largest church in South Korea and has over 700,000 members.[6] And he has this to say about India:

India has been called the cradle of the world's religions, having given birth to Hinduism, Buddhism, Jainism, and Sikhism. Yet today this land of exotic Eastern religions is also the home of over 60 million Christians. . . . many missiologists predict that by the year 2050 India will have over 100 million Christians.[7]

Today there are over 420,000 missionaries working around the world, but only 12 to 15 percent of them are from the West.[8] All of these statistics are good news because they prove that the church isn't dying after all. It's just no longer composed of only white Westerners.

"CHRISTIAN" IS A CURSE WORD

In the Middle East, Christian missionaries are creatively and humbly working in a region that truly is anti-Christian. In an article titled "Unlocking Islam: What a Kuwaiti Muslim 'Knows' about 'Christianity,'" Robby Butler tells of a Kuwaiti Muslim who learned as a young teen "that Christianity promoted immorality, pornography and television programs like *Dallas*." Butler goes on to write, "For a Muslim to say he has become a 'Christian' is to communicate that he has launched into a secret life of immorality."[9]

In Kuwait becoming a Christian is seen as entering into a prayer-less, apostate community. What they have done, like so many of us, is linked Christianity and America. From their perspective, America is a Christian nation and also the number one contributor to the pornography industry. Therefore, they attribute the downfall of global morality to this so-called "Christian America." Why would they want to become Christians?

What's interesting is they hold a very positive view of Jesus Christ. And these perceptions have caused some followers of Jesus in the Muslim community to remain in the mosque rather than unite with the Christian church. So how does a missionary living and ministering in a foreign land go about discipling a Muslim Christian? Well, you do it humbly, respectfully, and with much grace. You contextualize the environment and live with the awareness that the culture in which you are working and ministering in is not open to your faith. As youth workers, we must do the same thing.

Recently I was hanging out in a coffee shop with a group of adults who aren't from my church but who are becoming my friends. I say "becoming" because when they heard I was a pastor, huge walls went up. It wasn't like, "Oh, let's watch what we say in front of the pastor." It was much more antagonistic than that. For two years they've tried to get me mad, angry, or defensive. And I've tried to navigate and pursue a relationship with a group of people who deem me as being ignorant, bigoted, and backward just because I call myself a Christian. They aren't benevolent or kindhearted about my faith. So while it hasn't been easy for me, it's been good practice. Instead of trying to get them to sympathize with my faith, I suppose I've tried to sympathize with theirs.

Students don't want to be called Christians because of the baggage that comes with the title. They'll say things like, "Brock, if I become a Christian, then doesn't that mean I'll have to be pro-gun, anti-gay, and a Republican?" To this new post-Christian world, the word *Christian* is truly a curse word. And to many, it's almost synonymous with *Nazi*. How can this be? How do you lead students to a faith when it has a reputation like that? This, my friends, is a difficult world to minister in and navigate. But we've been called and selected and chosen for such a time as this.

Now for sure this characterization of Christians isn't
completely fair. One time I was talking with a girl in my youth
group who told me she hated Christians. She said they were
bigots and ignorant and full of hate. Honestly, I was offended
by her words. I mean, a Christian woman in our church was
mentoring this girl; a Christian family had intervened on her
behalf and rescued her from a terribly dysfunctional situation;
our church had rallied around her as many people in the
congregation took her shopping for new clothes and paid for
her to go to camp, on our mission trip, and on many retreats.
One family even bought her a new bicycle. Every Christian
she knew had loved her and treated her with thoughtful care
and kindness. Had she forgotten? Well, the answer is yes
and no. She hadn't forgotten the love and sacrifices of those
around her, but she is living in a culture that sees Christianity
as a terribly ugly thing. To many people, this is the Christian's
identity, and identity trumps everything. Even a new bicycle.

We need to maintain an awareness that we live in a post-
Christian culture. When the captives from the nation of Judah
entered Babylon, what they found was a city filled with
exiles from other nations. It was a city where many gods
were worshipped and where different codes of ethics were
followed. So think about this for a minute: What perspective,
view, and posture did the Israelites have while living in this
foreign land and pagan culture? Think of Daniel and his
quiet, humble, wise strength. What we see transpiring here
in Babylon is not altogether different from the ever-changing
cultural landscape in which we live today. Think of the
different cultures represented right here in our communities,
along with the various religious traditions that accompany

them. We must be thoughtful. We must be prayerful.
The trouble is that many churches, and many individual Christians, still believe that the prominent mindset in our culture is Christian.

Again, Christendom is over. So as followers of Jesus, we need to learn what it means to live as exiles in a culture that is not sympathetic to our faith. Being exiles is dangerous, and it needs prayerful and thoughtful responses. James understood this when he wrote, *"Everyone should be quick to listen, slow to speak and slow to become angry"* (James 1:19, NIV).

In America, we're starting to see that the majority of people who are sitting at the table do not agree with us. But instead of listening and being humble, we've just gotten louder. (Don't you hate it when people do that?) This response has created a negative reaction within our culture; and honestly, it hasn't kept this post-Christian world from emerging.

So what do we do? How will a post-Christian world impact our students? And what's the way forward?

CHAPTER TWO

A NEW WORLD'S IMPACT

I'm writing this chapter from Okemo Mountain in Vermont. I'm currently sitting on a deck that overlooks the valley. It's springtime, the snow is melting, the air is fresh, the pines are standing tall and green amidst the shorter flowering trees, and everywhere I look is full of wonder and beauty. It's an amazing view. Breathtaking. Sometimes you have to head up to the heights—to the summit view—to get some perspective, to take a look at life from a different vantage point, to see the big picture.

And then I received a phone call that brought me back down the mountain (figuratively speaking). The call was from a concerned father whose son went to camp with us this past summer and really connected with our youth group. Their family is fairly new to our church community, so the parents were relieved to see their son connect with our church. However, the son has slowly drifted away from our group since summer ended. He still comes about half the time, but he's not really there when he's there, ya know?

So back up the mountain I go to get some perspective. What is going on within this young man's world? What's influencing him? What's distracted him or caused him to be too busy and to pull away from us? And what are we leaders doing to lovingly allow him some space but not too much distance?

Environments have certain and specific outcomes. For example, if someone grows up in a dysfunctional home, that environment's continuous influence will shape a person's view of self and how he or she responds to people and certain situations. If a person lives in a safe, affirming, and nurturing environment, then it's more likely that he or she will have a strong sense of identity with a healthy sense of self.

Similarly, there are certain outcomes one can expect from living in a post-Christian world, and these are evident in the lives of our students. So with our bird's-eye view from the summit, let's take a broad look at what's influencing our students and ask, *Who are post-Christian students? What are they like and what are their assumptions?*

WELL-INFORMED AND INTELLIGENT

The first thing I notice from this height is that today's students are informed and intelligent. They've either read or been influenced by great agnostic writers such as Jorge Luis Borges, Betty Friedan, and Bart Ehrman. And if they have a question or need information, all they have to do is browse the Internet for answers.

When I was growing up, the teachers liked to assign book reports. But before I could begin working on my report, I had to walk two miles (in three feet of snow and uphill both ways, of course) to get to the library and search for the information I needed. Today, we live in a culture of immediate information. And that's not the only way things are different now.

Students take classes that teach them how to work in teams and how to listen to and respect each other's opinions. They also grapple with the kinds of questions I didn't even begin to deal with until I was in my early twenties. For many students, the end goal isn't high school graduation. They're already thinking about where they'll go to get their master's degrees. And they've been working on their college résumés since middle school. In high school these highly motivated students take advanced placement (AP) honors classes to earn college credit, which means many of them will eventually enter college with enough credits to make them sophomores. Even students who are growing up in communities where education isn't valued quite so highly are proving to be informed and thoughtful people.

During a conversation with one of our high school guys, he shared that in one of his classes, they were reading agnostic and atheistic thinkers, digesting them, and then debating as a group. He said he loved the class but felt really discouraged. Now, you have to understand that this young man is one of the highest-ranked students in his school, and his school is one of the most difficult in America. In fact, he'll attend an Ivy League college this fall. But you also need to know something else about him: He has a beautiful faith. He told me he's the only one in his class—including the teacher—who believes in a God. So for every point this student made during a discussion, the entire class had a counterpoint to make.

This is the world in which our students are growing up today, and they and their friends are no dummies. For Christian students with a faith that really matters to them, growing

up in a post-Christian world will cause them to feel like the
minority . . . *because they are.*

Thanks to the instant accessibility of information today, the
West has swiftly moved into a post-Christian world. It's as if
the world became flat, and now information comes flying at us
at about a hundred miles an hour. If you're a student, it's very
difficult to take in everything all at once. This is not to say that
information is the enemy; in fact, just the opposite. Because
of their knowledge, many students have a very thoughtful
faith and can actually explain what they believe and why. This
practice has given them a fairly strong foundation.

OVERLY STRESSED AND OVERSCHEDULED

What I've also noticed about student culture from the
summit view is how students today are overly stressed and
overscheduled. If you work with students, this shouldn't be a
surprise. But why is our world becoming so busy? In a post-
Christian world, no value is placed on the Sabbath, so our
children have some scheduled activity seven days a week.
This has created the most anxious and stressed-out generation
in history.

We recently had a meeting with our youth staff about what day
and time we should have our weekly youth group meetings.
We've been meeting on Sunday nights because that seems
to be the only free night students have each week. But now
even those nights are filling up with other activities. In our
community, regattas, practices, and games take up most of the
day on Sundays and on into the evening. When I was growing

up, the teachers at my school wouldn't assign as much homework on Wednesday nights so students could be involved in a church youth group. And sporting events, other than little league games, rarely occurred on a Saturday, but they never would have taken place on a Sunday.

The church and the family in this post-Christian world have been replaced with school and community activities seven days a week—with no breaks. If a student is active in school and interested in getting decent grades, then he or she probably has no block of time left unfilled. The day very well begins at 5 a.m. and often doesn't end until after midnight. A student might play on three sports teams during the school year, take college-bound honors classes, and all while working 20 hours a week at a local Hollister. They are truly busy and can't imagine being anything else. And all the while their parents applaud this hectic pace of life.

While riding in a car with one of our recent graduates, I asked how it felt to be done with high school. He said he was completely relieved because his high school years had been "beyond stressful." He said, "I can't imagine college being as stressful, and it just can't be! It better not be!" I asked him what advice he'd give to a high school freshman who are heading into these demanding and powerless years. He said, "Just knuckle down and get through it."

I was really surprised by his answer. So I followed up with, "You wouldn't do it any differently?"

He said, "You can't; there's nothing you can do. We have no

control." Wow! Students today can't even imagine a different way to live.

T. S. Eliot once wrote that we are "distracted from distraction by distraction." The days of getting students to attend multiple youth functions in the same week are long gone, let alone getting them to attend a couple of times a month. Oswald Chambers writes in *My Utmost for His Highest*, "The greatest enemy of the life of faith in God is not sin, but good choices which are not quite good enough. The good is always the enemy of the best."[10]

So just as Florida and Arizona have an annual snowbird season (when senior citizens head south for the winter months), I bet you have students who disappear for seasons at a time as well. Band season. SAT season. Soccer season. Play season. You get the picture.

Adults might be tempted to assume that kids' lives are happy-go-lucky and full of downtime. However, the results of a 2006 KidsHealth® KidsPoll showed that of the 882 kids ages 9 to 13 who were surveyed, 41 percent reported feeling stressed either "most of the time" or "always" because they had too much to do.[11] In fact colleges are finding that incoming freshmen are the most stressed-out students in history. In 2011, researchers at UCLA surveyed more than 200,000 incoming freshmen who "reported all-time lows in overall mental health and emotional stability."[12]

If you sit across the table from a middle school student, you'll be alarmed to hear about the stress he or she is carrying. And the weight of the world just gets heavier with each passing year. Ask your students what causes them to feel distant from God. I guarantee you that busyness will be at the top of the list. They're just too busy. They are overwhelmed by their schoolwork, by their friendships, by their activities, and by their family life.

Last fall a girl from our youth group called and asked if she could meet with me as soon as possible. So she came to my house, we sat on my back porch, and she began telling me that she'd been having panic attacks. (If you've never had a panic attack, then you should know that the sufferer feels like he or she is having a heart attack. You have difficulty breathing, your heart pounds, and you honestly believe you're going to die.) She told me she'd been having these attacks about three times a week. Initially she didn't think it was a big deal because "all of her friends have them."

When you have a panic attack, your body and mind are telling you they've had enough. Enough work, enough stress, enough fear, enough busyness—ENOUGH! So obviously this girl's psyche had had enough. I told her we needed to get her some counseling, which we did. I told her she needed to cut back on her workload, which she didn't do. She felt like she couldn't drop anything. In her mind, everything on her to-do list was "vital." Students today feel the weight of the world on their shoulders. They are overscheduled and stressed-out. So what does this mean for how we program? If we program? What does this mean in terms of what we work on with the parents? Maybe in the future the church should become a place of rest and restoration.

FIGHTING FOR CONTROL

But in the midst of this overscheduled existence, what you'll find are students who are fighting for what little control they can get. When you feel like you can't say no to anything, what do you do? You see, a post-Christian world will overschedule you. The Judeo-Christian principle of sabbath is dismissed. There is no free time, no days off, no relaxed evenings, and nothing is optional. Teachers overload you with homework, and if you don't get it all done and do a great job, it could very well jeopardize your future.

I had a conversation with a mom who told me her son, a sixth grade boy, was overwhelmed and full of anxiety because he felt an enormous amount of pressure to complete all of his homework with excellence. Now, he isn't a bookworm kind of a kid. He loves sports, youth group, and hanging out with his friends. But he is gripped by a fear of disappointing his teacher. But it's not just teachers, it's coaches, and clubs, and you name it. Nothing is optional today. You must be at everything.

So think about it: if you're an adolescent, then you're probably looking to take back some control. And that means you need to say no to something. This is called the process of individuation, and every adolescent must go through it. As you get older, it's natural that you'll pull away from authority, especially your parents', and try to figure out if you have any power—if your choices matter. But you only feel comfortable saying no to church, to youth group, and even to God. So that's what you do. You think, *That'll teach my parents who's boss! I'll just say no to going to church, and that will give me some more control over my life—at least in one area.*

In a post-Christian world, saying no to church is the last acceptable option. One student shared how he told his school's guidance counselor about all of the stress he's been feeling and how overwhelmed he's been. Now, this kid is super-involved. He's participating in clubs and sports, taking honor classes, performing in plays . . . you name it, he's involved in it. So when he went over his schedule with the guidance counselor, she told him he needed to cut back on youth group—that was his only option.

A friend told me he'd read that not long ago Germany was intrigued by the American educational system. Historically, elementary school for German children was built around long periods of play with intermittent times of education, while American educational structures are the opposite—work all day with maybe 30 minutes of recess and a 30-minute lunch break. Once Germany tried the "American way," they found it had no benefits. The children didn't learn any more than they had before. In fact, they became more stressed, and the number of behavioral problems increased. This makes me want to climb into Doc's DeLorean time machine, travel back in time, and move to Germany (à la *Back to the Future*).

STARBUCKS SPIRITUALITY

The next thing we see from this height is that teenagers tend to personalize their spirituality, and it can become a pick-and-choose proposition. It's like ordering something at Starbucks, "I'll take a Grande Caramel Kabbalah Latte with a shot of

Buddhism, and a Hindu Krishna cookie on the side." This kind of "Starbucks spirituality" is not an easy environment to minister in when everything is on the table. If you aren't in the mood for a Venti Buddhist Meditation, then why not try a Tall Jesus during the retreat this weekend?

A couple of years ago, I had the pleasure of leading a girl in my youth group to the Lord. When she met Christ, a dramatic change occurred within her. It was as if God hadn't just saved her soul, but he'd rescued her personality as well. But as with most adolescents, over time her spiritual walk began to look more like a roller coaster than a stable foundation. She'd feel close to God one week and then have serious doubts about his existence the next. As her youth workers and her biggest fans, we just kept spending time with her, listening, encouraging, and praying with her.

In the midst of this back-and-forth, up-and-down journey of hers, I flew out to San Diego to speak at the National Youth Workers Convention and talk about the post-Christian world that I was ministering in out in New England. It was an amazing time of hanging out with and encouraging youth workers from all over the country.

I'm going to pause this story for just a moment and let you in on a little secret: If a youth ministry speaker doesn't work with students between his or her speaking engagements, it's easy for that person to forget just how difficult ministry can be. And one might feel inclined to believe that he or she has it all figured out. Sometimes I start to feel that way even after just one weekend of speaking. But then I return home to my students who live with a Starbucks spirituality, and I am humbled and back on my knees.

So I finished speaking at the National Youth Workers Convention, flew home, and soon after that this newly saved girl called and said she wanted to tell me something exciting. So we're sitting in Starbucks (which I thought was pretty appropriate) when she drops this bomb on me: "Brock, while you were away, I became a Buddhist!" She even said it with a peppy attitude. If she assumed I'd think this was a good thing, she found out pretty quickly that I wasn't very happy about it. Exhausted after traveling across the country, I was not on my A-game. She asked, "Does this bother you?" I wanted to say, "Hell yes, it bothers me!" But I got it together and started asking her questions—but not loaded questions. I asked where Jesus fit into all of this. She hadn't thought about that, but then she asked if she could be a Buddhist Christian. I wasn't sure how to respond, so I acted like her question was rhetorical.

Here's the deal: this is the world our kids are growing up in, and they need to feel safe as they study, research, and try on different faiths. But this Starbucks spirituality is a growing trait, and it's something we need to really think through. In a post-Christian world, you're going to hear this kind of stuff. You're going to hear that students consider themselves "Buddhist Christians" and a plethora of other mashups. How are you going to respond? As students explore the flat world we live in with all of its options spread out like a buffet line, how we respond could make all the difference in the world.

A LIFE WORTH LIVING

Next, from our high vantage point we see that students are dying to have a life worth living. They see the world, which doesn't seem so far away anymore, and they truly want to make a difference in it. They want to write amazing stories with their lives.

George Gallup Jr. says this about today's students:

> *America's teenagers see themselves contributing to a better world in the new century upon us—a world with less racial discrimination, a world more concerned about the needs of the less fortunate, a world that is less polluted and more caring about the environment, a more peaceful world with fewer wars and armed conflicts. And finally, teenagers see themselves contributing to a world of new hope and sense of purpose.*[13]

As a 23-year veteran youth worker, I can tell you that I am sick to death of pie-in-the-face games. Don't get me wrong, I love *watching* them; but don't ask me to lead one or participate in it. I'm also sick to death of talking about faith and doctrine while not living it out as a community. About a year ago, I stood up during youth group and said how tired I was of sitting in that room and talking about the faith. I said I wanted to get out there and actually *do* the faith; I wanted to make a difference in the world. I told them I was going to start meeting with whoever wanted to join me on Sunday nights, and we were going to actually *do* the faith.

After that, more kids started coming on Sunday nights than on Wednesday nights. They all felt tired of "youth group." They wanted to make a difference. They wanted their faith to matter in the real world. So we're now in the process of launching a nonprofit called Mission 220 that's owned and operated by our students. The name comes from Galatians 2:20—"*I have been crucified with Christ and I no longer live, but Christ lives in me. The life I now live in the body, I live by faith in the Son of God, who loved me and gave himself for me*" (NIV).

In the beginning, our students set some goals that we wanted to accomplish within the first couple of years. The first was to partner with other organizations and help rescue children from slavery. We sent a few high school kids to the International Justice Mission (IJM) in Guatemala to investigate our options and report back to the group. They also made connections with an organization in Cambodia, raised some money, and now we're about to take part in our first rescue. Other students in the group are managing local missions and planning a local mission trip for the summer. They are doing it, they are passionate about it, and I don't have to get a pie smashed in my face.

What if our youth ministries became places where students could actually make a difference in the world—and not just once a year in Mexico? We'll talk more about this later.

SHALLOW AND CONSUMERISTIC

We notice a few other things from this mountaintop view. We see that even in the midst of their longing to bring deep change into the world, students are still shallow and consumeristic. This post-Christian world targets them with massive advertising campaigns and a media onslaught. Because of this never-ending push to get teens to consume, our students have fallen for it hook, line, and sinker, believing they really must have the "right" headphones, T-shirts, and shoes that everyone else has—particularly their friends.

However, they don't buy just a product; they buy an *experience*. Our students want active interaction, not passive purchasing. For instance, teens will have no problem spending $60 on a pair of TOMS shoes because for every pair of TOMS shoes that are purchased, the company gives a pair of shoes to needy people around the world. By purchasing a pair of TOMS, teens feel like they're changing the world, but at the same time they're remaining very fashionable.

The desire for this type of interaction extends to their food purchases as well. Several students at a camp asked me if the chicken we were serving them was organic and locally grown. I told them the chicken was certainly local . . . somewhere. And this desire also bleeds into their spiritual life. Spirituality is often seen as a source of personal satisfaction that can help them feel better about their stressful lives; it's not about kingdom advancement at all.

I wonder how we youth leaders have contributed to this view? In the past, sometimes I've felt less like a pastor or a shepherd and more like a used car salesman. (I sincerely apologize to any used car salesmen who are reading this right now.) Have we made youth ministry just another product for teens to consume? How do we market our youth ministries? Do we come across as inauthentic? Overly slick? Do we pull a bait-and-switch on them?

In his book *Working the Angels*, Eugene Peterson says, "The pastors of America have metamorphosed into a company of shopkeepers, and the shops they keep are churches. They are preoccupied with shopkeepers' concerns—how to keep the customers happy, how to lure costumers away from competitors down the street, how to package the goods so that the customers will lay out more money."[14] Ouch!

But students are also overwhelmed by the shallowness of all things. Their heroes have been getting plastic surgery for years, and now even teenagers can have those body parts that they feel are "lacking in some way" augmented, nipped, tucked, or reduced. "According to American Society of Plastic Surgeons (ASPS) statistics, nearly 219,000 cosmetic plastic surgery procedures were performed on people age 13-19 in 2010. These surgeries included 35,000 nose jobs and 8,500 breast augmentations performed on 18-to-19-year-olds."[15] And according to a press release from the American Society for Aesthetic Plastic Surgery (ASAPS), "In 2012 there were 3,576 breast augmentation procedures performed on women 18 and under, 1.1% percent of the total number of breast augmentation procedures." And 52 percent of those procedures were simply cosmetic bilateral breast augmentations. In other words, there was no medical necessity for the surgery.[16] Although in recent years there has been a downswing in the number of cosmetic surgeries being performed on teens (probably due to the economic downturn), we are seeing the shallowness of all things consuming our students.

I once overheard a fifth grade girl refuse a donut, saying, "Really, I shouldn't." With eating disorders on the rise among teens, and with kids feeling "humiliated" because their moms bought them the wrong color Uggs, the shallow, narcissistic atmosphere of our world is getting pretty tough for our students to breathe; it's basically suffocating them. What's going on?

Social media has really contributed to this problem, starting with Myspace, then Facebook, and now Instagram—anyplace online where you can present "the best version" of yourself to others. Blogger Sarah Brooks explains it well in her post entitled "Parents: A Word about Instagram":

We're no longer in world of handwritten "circle yes or no" notes between two people; your kids are living social lives on a completely public forum.

This is not new information.

*But, taking it a step further: have you considered that your child is given **numerical values** on which to base his or her social standing? For the first time ever your children can determine their "worth" using <u>actual numbers</u> provided by their peers!*

Let me explain . . .

Your daughter has 139 followers which is 23 less than Jessica, but 56 more than Beau. Your son's photo had 38 likes which was 14 less than Travis' photo, but 22 more than Spencer's.

See what I mean? There's a number attached to them. A ranking.[17]

Do you see what's happening? Teenagers are definitely paying attention to the culture around them (which is what teenagers have always done), and it's affecting them for sure. But it's not just about *assumed* popularity anymore. It's explicit. It's quantifiable. At the most difficult time in their lives—a crucial time of development when they're trying to figure out who they are and where they belong and if they have any power in this world—this is the kind of stuff they're up against. A scientific means for measuring popularity. (#5newfollowers, #81likes, #iamsopopular)

I was talking about this issue with my wife one day. She admitted that while she really wanted to be popular when she was in middle school, she's been surprised to see just how obsessed with popularity her small group of seventh grade girls are. Teens get their feelings hurt when popular kids "like" the pictures above and below theirs on the Instagram news feed, but not their photos. They delete pictures of themselves when they don't get as many "likes" as they were hoping for. They don't get invited to parties, yet they can still look at all of the photos that are posted from those events—and see all of the fun they missed out on. They'll even post ugly pictures of their friends as a way to get revenge.

This is a brand-new element in the slow cooker that we call

"culture," and it will be interesting to watch its impact over the next decade or two. But it's definitely contributing to our shallow world today.

ADDICTED

One of the most troubling things about the lives of post-Christian students is they come to us addicted. On a recent middle school retreat, I noticed a sixth grade boy sitting by himself and not participating in the game. We'd just finished the evening program, so I figured he was feeling moved by the message or something. I asked him if everything was okay. With his head down, he said he was feeling really ashamed of himself. I asked if he wanted to talk about it, and he told me he wasn't ready. But on the following night, he walked up and asked me if we could talk. He began telling me how when he was in fourth grade, he and his friends had started looking at porn. At first it seemed fun and harmless, but now he just felt stuck. He said he hated it, but he couldn't stop looking at it; he didn't know what to do. By now he was sobbing and could barely get the words out. I was crying right there with him. And then he collapsed into my arms like the little boy he is.

Philip G. Zimbardo, professor emeritus of psychology at Stanford University, has done extensive research about the porn industry and its effects on teenage guys. His data shows that boys are 30 percent more likely to flunk out of school than girls, boys make up two-thirds of all special ed students, and boys are five times more likely to have ADHD. Zimbardo says a leading contributor to all of the problems boys have today is a fear of intimacy, a fear of having a physical and emotional connectedness with someone else. He goes on to say, "Boys now prefer a synchronistic Internet world to the spontaneous interaction of social relationships." He says this is caused by excessive Internet use in general, excessive video gaming, and more specifically the alarming rates of viewing new pornographic material. In other words, it's all due to arousal addiction—the need for not just more of something, but *more* and different. They're addicted to *novelty*. He also says boys today are watching 50 pornographic video clips per week. Did you get that?[18]

We obviously have a crisis on our hands. What a difficult world to grow up in! But this isn't just a guy thing.

While speaking at a youth camp a couple of summers ago, one night I talked about confession. At the end of my talk, I invited anyone in the audience who felt led to do so to come up to the microphone and say something, get something off their chests, confess. Now, in hindsight this might not have been the best idea. However, a teenage girl came forward and stood beside me. She was crying before she even grabbed the mic. I'd noticed her throughout the week; she looked fun, she was pretty, and she seemed confident but a bit withdrawn. And now here she was stammering and crying in front of a thousand high school kids as she began confessing her porn addiction. I couldn't believe it. This was social suicide for a young girl. But what happened next blew me away. Girls came running to the front and surrounded her. They were all crying and praying and supporting each other. Later that night in the cabins, female leaders heard all about the secret lives of teenage girls.

Of course sexual addiction isn't the only type of addiction teenagers wrestle with; there are all kinds of traps for students to fall into these days:

- The average age when youth first try alcohol is 11 years for boys and 13 years for girls.
- The average age at which Americans begin drinking regularly is 15.9 years old.
- Teens who start drinking before age 15 are five times more likely to develop alcohol dependence or abuse later in life than those who begin drinking at or after the legal age of 21.
- It has been estimated that over three million teenagers are out-and-out alcoholics. Several million more have a serious drinking problem that they cannot manage on their own.
- The three leading causes of death for 15-to-24-year-olds are automobile crashes, homicides, and suicides— alcohol is a leading factor in all three.[19]

The average age of first marijuana use in America is 14, and it's the most prevalent drug used by teens and young adults. We've all heard students joke about marijuana being a gateway drug. But the truth is, it's a gateway into a lifestyle of compromises. Addiction and substance abuse have different faces in this generation. It's not just the druggies and burnouts who are using. Drug use is becoming a norm, and we're finding that some of our "best kids" are falling into this destructive pattern.

When you grow up in a world that glorifies things that are dangerous, it becomes difficult to know what's right or wrong, what's beneficial or destructive. During a youth group gathering this past spring, I spoke about the rich young ruler and how he believed in Jesus and had experienced Jesus, but he wasn't willing to actually *follow* Jesus (Matthew 19:16-22; Mark 10:17-27). A senior guy came up to me to ask for prayer afterward, and he told me he wasn't ready to follow Jesus either. He wasn't willing to give up the random hookups, the one-night stands, and the party scene. He really believed his way was much better than God's way. This response is nothing new. It's an ancient dilemma that plagued Adam, King Saul, Simon Peter, the rich young ruler, me, you, and all of our students.

But today, even if teenagers *want* to honor God with their choices, they struggle to do so because they're caught in the grip of heavy addictions from such a young age. They're wrapped up in destructive patterns and habits and lifestyles. If you follow Jesus, then what in the world are you supposed to do on Saturday nights? This young man has a really good heart. He *wanted* to follow Jesus, but he ended up walking away feeling sad and stuck, and with no moral imagination. Like Jesus, I just had to let him go, and I felt a pit form in my stomach. Yet I know his story is far from over.

LOOKING FOR SOMETHING BIGGER THAN THEMSELVES

In the midst of all the dust kicked up by a post-Christian world, we see students who are looking for a movement. They really do want a faith that is meaningful, and they want to be a part of something much bigger than themselves. They want a spiritual life and a spiritual experience that can take them out of this everyday world and blow their minds with something so big that they have a hard time putting words to it.

Over the Labor Day weekend in 2012, 110,000 people— mostly young people—participated in the fourth-annual Electric Zoo, an electronic music festival and rave that's held just outside of New York City. As the students move together to the music, they experience feelings like they've never had before. Even if it's just for a night, they feel like they are a part of something bigger than themselves. Teenagers who are seeking a vast movement will find it wherever they can—and those places and experiences can be healthy or unhealthy, helpful or hurtful. In fact, during the 2013 EZoo Festival, two people died from a suspected drug overdose on the drug MOLLY (ecstasy), and at least four others were hospitalized and in critical condition in the ICU, leading the event organizers to cancel the final day of the three-day festival. Now the cancellation of one day of one music festival might not seem like a big deal. But for students, even the unhealthy and eventually hurtful experiences "feel like something," so teenagers are drawn to them. This means our students can easily get caught up in big social movements. If you look back in history, you'll find that teenagers were often at the forefront of movements like the civil rights struggle, tent revival meetings, and the Great Awakenings.

The cool thing is that God clearly has a revolution in mind. Jesus came to inaugurate a new kingdom, a new idea that was bigger than anything before it—including the Roman Empire. All of history, from creation to the end, is moving toward the fulfillment of God's plan. So the questions we should be asking are, *What does God want our students to be doing right now? What battle should they be giving their lives to, what injustice should they be bringing light to, what evil should they banish? What revolution should they be joining?*

The answers might be within you. For me, it was sex trafficking and slavery around the world. Little girls and boys being forced to do unspeakable things—I want to shed a light on that; I want to right that wrong. And God has called me to get students to help me in that cause. Maybe God has called you to be a person of justice and placed specific students around you so you can show them the way of Jesus, how to be his hands and feet, be his voice of hope. Your students long to do something radical in the world. They long to be a part of a movement. And maybe you're the one God has appointed to turn your youth group into a mission. Maybe then your students will know what to do with their Saturday nights.

So I sit here on this deck at Mt. Okemo that overlooks the valley. From my vantage point, I can breathe and see both the good and the bad. I can look at the trees and see which way the wind is blowing. I love summit views. I love being in the heights and getting a new perspective. But now it's time to head back to the valley and do some work.

CHAPTER THREE

THE WAY OF THE SAGE

While I was driving one day, I accidently turned on a Christian radio station. These are hard to find where I live, but somehow I stumbled upon one. And the reason I kept listening to it was because an author was being interviewed about teenagers growing up in a pluralistic society. This topic obviously grabbed my attention, but the man's suggestion for how to help students keep their faith seemed shortsighted and simplistic. It was so frustrating, in fact, that I actually found myself yelling at the radio at times.

The author said teenagers struggle so much today because they aren't being taught the Bible. Right away I cynically thought, *I bet this guy hasn't worked with teenagers for 20 years*. He then confirmed my suspicion, "When I was a youth pastor in the '80s, we just taught the Bible and that was enough." He went on to talk about how we need to teach students that when the Bible says God created the world in six days, it means six literal days. He said, "We have to teach the inerrancy of Scripture; this will solve our problems."

Many years ago I spoke about the reliability of Scripture, how the Christian faith is reasonable, and Jesus is the only way to God. Afterward, a young teenage guy came up to me and said, "What you just taught us kind of makes sense, but you seemed angry while you were speaking. Are you upset with us?" Well, this guy on the radio reminded me of myself when I was 23: simplistic, shortsighted, reactionary, insecure, and disrespectful to varying viewpoints.

What youth workers are dealing with today is extremely complex. If the solution to the world's problems was teaching the Bible, then my students shouldn't have any problems growing up in today's world because I *do* teach Scripture. However, youth ministry has never been about giving information; it's about so much more than that. The world needs great youth workers who will teach students *how* to think, not spoon-feed them *what* to think. We need savvy youth workers who will journey with kids in today's complex world and teach them how to humbly engage in the culture's toughest questions. Why? Because our students are asking the exact same questions. Youth workers need to be great tour guides, pointing out things that kids would have missed otherwise.

When I was 18 years old, I headed off to college with dreams and fears and an array of conflicting and beautiful ideas. At the time I felt a bit lost and needed someone to come alongside me, to journey with me. I needed a mentor, a sage to lovingly give me wisdom and vision and help me discover who I really was. Instead, about two weeks into my college experience, I found myself getting kicked out of school. Now, keep in mind that this was a conservative Christian college, and I didn't think the rules applied to me. (Actually, I still kind of think that way today.)

So there I was, sitting in the office of the dean of students. He was preparing to sign my dismissal papers when in walked Mr. Ropp, one of my professors. Mr. Ropp asked the dean if he could speak with him for a moment, and the two of them had a heated conversation in the hallway. I couldn't make out exactly what they were saying, but I knew they were talking about me. After a few minutes, the dean walked back in, ripped the papers in half, and said, "You're not getting kicked out of school, but you'll need to meet with Mr. Ropp every week for the next couple of months." I breathed a sigh of relief and gave Mr. Ropp a huge bear hug. As I met with him, Mr. Ropp was the first person to play the role of a sage in my life. His display of grace drew me back to reengaging in a spiritual life.

Soon after that, God brought another man into my life—a sage who changed my life's trajectory. Dr. Bill Brown was the president of the school, and one day he asked me if some of my friends and I would be willing to meet with him every Thursday morning. Of course I said yes. So for the next four years, Dr. Brown met with us, invested in us, and called us out of normalcy.

One Thursday morning he looked at each of us and asked, "Do you guys know why we're doing this? Do you know why I'm meeting with you every week?" (Have you ever been asked a question where you know the answer should be obvious, but you really don't have a clue what the answer is? That's how I felt in this moment.) We all just stared at Dr. Brown with blank expressions. He continued, "Well, I'm not meeting with you because I want you to become great men. You already *are* great men. And I'm not meeting with you because I want you to believe in Jesus. You already believe in Jesus. I'm meeting with you because I see something remarkable in each of you. I see young men who could bring such amazing change to this world." These kinds of conversations always blow my mind. But no one had ever spoken to me like this before—except maybe my father. And honestly, it was ruining everything for me.

You see, I was a PE major—not because I wanted to help bring healthy exercise habits to children around the country. I just wanted to play dodgeball for the rest of my life. But the way Dr. Brown spoke to us caused me to rethink this whole dodgeball career idea. So one day I asked, "Dr. Brown, what do you see in me? What do you think I should be doing with my life? Because what you've been teaching us is totally screwing up my whole plan."

Without hesitating he said, "Brock, you'd be a great youth pastor." When he said it, I honestly think he was levitating or something because his words seemed to come right from the mouth of God. I immediately knew that youth ministry was exactly what I was supposed to do with my life. That was in the spring of 1991, and the very next day I started volunteering in a Young Life type club. (And the cool thing is that I still get to play dodgeball!)

That's what sages do—*they lovingly see the people around them with God's eyes.* They have a vision. Sages live extraordinary lives, and they invite the younger generations along for the ride. They are the keepers of beautiful questions and life-altering stories. They aren't threatened by opposing ideas, but they engage in conversation and contribute to the shaping of hearts and minds.

When my wife and I saw the movie *Life of Pi*, I absolutely loved it. I was especially struck by the multilayered narrative. At every turn I kept seeing the gospel and was moved by how God was shown to be so much bigger than my own personal religion. The movie begins with a writer interviewing the main character, Pi Patel, who's a sage. Pi wanted to know what his friend Mamaji had already told the writer about Pi. The writer says, "He said you had a story that will make me believe in God." Now, he's not talking about religion here; Pi has a story that will help open up this writer's life to a new way, a better way. This person's paradigm is about to be shifted, altered.

Pi laughs and says, "He would say that about a nice meal. As for God, I can only tell you my story. You'll decide for yourself what you believe."

A sage trusts an individual's journey. More importantly, a sage trusts the Holy Spirit to work in a person's life. There is no fear. Unfortunately, a lot of my youth ministry has been done with a hint of fear. I've been afraid that kids might have premarital sex, that a student might leave the faith, that other students might experiment with drugs, that a student might land on the wrong theology, that students won't like me, that the program won't draw many students, that my talk won't be funny, that parents might get mad, or that I might lose my job. However, fear is never from God. (Except for the fear of God, of course, but that's a different story.) A sage doesn't allow fear to dictate his or her ministry. Trust in the Lord beats out fear in the life of a sage every time. So when a student *does* leave the faith, a sage's heart is filled with a hopeful reliance on the Holy Spirit to bring that person back.

About a year ago, I received a text that simply read: HAVE YOU SEEN BRIAN'S FACEBOOK POST YET? I hadn't, so I quickly clicked over and saw that he'd just posted that he was no longer a follower of Jesus. He'd also unfriended me and dropped out of our youth group's Facebook page. I quickly sent a message to tell him that if he ever wanted to talk, get together, or hang out, he should let me know. He responded kind of awkwardly and made it clear that he just wanted space. A couple of days later, the other students asked if we could have a time of prayer for Brian during youth group. It was amazing! Kids all over that room were proclaiming their trust in God. They knew that doubt comes in and can overwhelm a person at times. So they simply prayed that God would gently lead Brian back—back to himself and to our youth group. It was really cool to see and hear our students lifting up a friend in prayer. And I believe what set the atmosphere that day was how we leaders, as sages, had responded. We set the tone of trust, calm, and no fear—just faith. Sages lead the way.

A sage isn't afraid of disagreement. I love the old Robert Frost quote, "You are educated when you have the ability to listen to almost anything without losing your temper or self-confidence." Back when I was in third grade, I witnessed three men yelling at each other in a Pizza Hut one Sunday night. I asked my father why the two men were yelling at the other one. My dad said, "Well, they want that fella over there to become a Christian, but he won't." That's when I first realized that yelling and arguing probably aren't the best evangelistic methods. In fact, I don't think I've ever seen anyone come to faith because they lost an argument.

Many years ago there was a student in my youth group whose last name was Fight. Seriously, it was Fight. And boy, did he fight me on everything. He battled with me about the games we played, the songs we sung, and the topics of all of my talks. Everything was a fight to young Mr. Fight. Soon, I began to fear him. I'd write my talks in fear, wondering what he would do or say afterward. Plus, it wasn't unusual for Fight to interrupt my talks with loaded questions and heat-seeking missiles. To be honest, I think I started to hate Fight. I guess it was really more of a love-hate relationship: Fight loved to get me flustered, and I hated his face.

There was an older volunteer leader who absolutely loved Fight. This leader saw something in Fight that the kid didn't see in himself. To be honest, he saw something in Fight that none of the rest of us saw. He looked at Fight and saw a deep thinker, a young rebel leader who could bring depth to shallowness. He knew that given enough time and investment, young Fight could be a kingdom mover. This volunteer leader was a sage, and he'd sit next to Fight during youth group and allow Fight to be himself. (To be honest, I found this a little annoying.) But in the end, the leader was right. Fight was a natural leader, and he would become a great and mighty man.

A sage lives an extraordinary life. He or she is full of life experience and truly lives every day. I've had some elderly heroes in my life. Of course, I've also known many grumpy old men and women, but once in a while you run into an amazing elderly person. And every one of them, across the board, has lived a beautiful narrative. They have many years under their belts of living life well, following Jesus into dark and scary places, and turning the daily mundane into a beautiful stillness.

In my early twenties, I wandered into a bookstore one day and ended up in the magazine aisle. I soon found myself gravitating toward the "naughty" magazine section where I bumped into this grizzled, seventy-something gentleman, "Excuse me, sir," I said. Then I noticed he was looking at a *Hustler.* I immediately felt ill and thought, *God, I'm no better than that guy. Help me not to become that kind of man!* And start changing me now! We all know men and women we don't want to be like. But occasionally you'll come across the cream of the crop, a sage, someone who has lived, as Eugene Peterson wrote, *a long obedience in the same direction.*

So how are you living? Where are you at right now? What's going on in your mind, behind closed doors, or in the magazine aisle? The next generation is desperate for sages to come alongside them with years of beautiful living, years of beautiful choices. They've heard enough "what not to do" stories. They need sages who can show them how to live well.

A sage sees life from all sides and angles. He or she doesn't see life as black or white; a sage's favorite color is grey. I was riding in the car with a recent seminary grad when he made this statement, "Anyone who thinks like that has to be an idiot and is definitely not a Christian!" He was talking about a particular viewpoint on government policy. And the funny thing is that he was criticizing my own personal leaning without even knowing it. Instead of debating or shaming him, I stayed quiet and waited for an opportunity to speak humble truth and widen his perspective. But that moment never came. His seminary had taught him a worldview that didn't allow for alternative perspectives. So I just changed the subject.

Students today need to be let off the hook. They need to know it's okay to have a differing opinion. They must know that they can belong before they ever believe—Christians have all kinds of perspectives and viewpoints, and it's okay. In fact, it's beautiful that the faith is broad and there's enough room for all of us. See, a sage can understand why another person could think the way he or she thinks, even if it's the complete opposite of what the sage believes. A sage respects and even enjoys opposing opinions. With a bold curiosity, he or she engages and is always learning.

From the time I was a little boy, my parents have written notes about the things I've said. I remember coming home from college and telling my parents what I was learning in a particular class. They both ran off to get something to write on, so they could take notes of my "brilliant" 19-year-old mind. The amazing thing is they weren't faking it. They were always ready to learn and grow and be stretched. That's a sage, and it's who God calls us to be. I love James 1:19—"*My dear brothers and sisters, take note of this: Everyone should be quick to listen, slow to speak and slow to become angry"* (NIV).

A sage lives by the "me too" principle. As a newly wedded man, my character flaws began to surface more and more. Before I got married, there were things in my life that I'd never dealt with, and I naively thought marriage would fix me. (Have you ever made that mistake?) So I got on a plane and flew out to meet with Dr. Bill Brown once again. I wanted to confess, and I needed some direction and wisdom. When I arrived at his office, I got right to it. There was no time for small talk; I was too desperate. So I laid it all on the table, withholding nothing. I told him all of my struggles and how marriage was bringing out the worst in me.

I'm not sure what I expected Dr. Brown to do after I unloaded on him. Maybe offer a disapproving look or at least a, "Wow, Brock, I'm sorry you're going through this." But that's not what he did. Instead, he looked me in the eyes and said, "Brock, *me too.* I am desperate for Jesus too. I need Jesus too." Then he got on his knees and invited me to join him so we could pray for each other. I walked out of his office feeling oddly awesome. I felt free. I felt like I had a companion in this struggle to follow Jesus in the details of my life.

In the Old Testament the prophets and men of God always identified with the people. They'd lower themselves and say prayers like, "*We* have sinned before you, we have turned our backs on you, and we have walked away from you, Lord!" When you're reading those portions of Scripture, you might think, *Wait a minute.* The people were the sinners. *The* people

turned their backs on God; you didn't. But sages identify
with the people, and they always see their own weaknesses.
Our lead pastor spoke about this one day. He said there are so
many horrible things he would have done if given the opportunity. Hmmm . . . me too.

Lastly, a sage has a heart for the next generation. I love the
psalmist's prayer, "*Even when I am old and gray, do not
forsake me, my God, till I declare your power to the next
generation, your mighty acts to all who are to come*" (Psalm
71:18, NIV). There is this desperate sense to always be telling
students about how great our God is. The psalmist's top
priority is to pass the faith on, to ensure that the movement
continues. And by the way, this is you. *You* have that heart;
you long to see young men and women live a life after Jesus.
This is *your* passion and your calling. This is why you can't
sleep at night because you carry the next generation so close
to your heart. And you're investing in them because you
believe they can do it. You, along with Jesus, actually believe
in them.

Sages are pioneers, teachers, adventurers, humorists, scientists, dreamers, and artists. They are visionaries living The
Way of Jesus in a culture that isn't. And this is you. And this
is me. What a divine calling we have to declare Christ's power
to the next generation. It is our mission to declare the Good
News, but not with veins popping from our necks or with a
narrow-minded arrogance. We get to brag on what God has
done and what he is doing. We get to listen and learn and trust.
We get to be his tender voice to a generation who is longing
for tenderness. We get to be his attentive, listening ear to a

generation who longs for a voice. Wow! I couldn't think of a better life!

CHAPTER FOUR

THE WAY FORWARD: A RESPONSE TO A POST-CHRISTIAN WORLD

Recently I sat on a park bench and had one of those amazing conversations with a high school guy. We talked about life, drugs, family, faith, and of course, sex. Ultimately he wanted to get a feel for me and my faith. His older brother, an agnostic, was in college. And big brother had heard that this young man had started going to some youth group. (To be more specific, he was going to my youth group—the one that's really into Jesus.) So he'd been giving his little brother a hard time about it. What I've learned over the years is that before students make a decision for Christ, they ask themselves, *Do I want to be like you and your friends?* I think that's what this high schooler was doing. He'd been coming to our group for a couple of months, and now he needed to evaluate what we were all about. Did he truly want to be like my friends and me?

Over the last couple of years, our group has taken students through Youth Alpha, an amazing program for 11-18 year-olds that was created by a spectacular church in London called Holy Trinity Brompton. The Alpha website says, "Alpha is a practical introduction to the Christian faith, aimed particularly at non-churchgoers and new Christians... Youth Alpha is designed to give young people . . . the opportunity to explore life and faith." (For more info, check out www.alpha.org or www.alphausa.org.) One of the videos we show during the Youth Alpha course is "Word on the Street." You've probably seen these types of videos before, but this one begins by asking random people what they think of Jesus. The cool thing is that almost across the board, everyone interviewed in the post-Christian city of London is extremely positive about Jesus. Everyone loves him.

However, when the question changes to "What do you think of Christians?" I'm sure you can guess some of the responses:

- Ignorant
- Bigoted
- Homophobic
- Hateful
- Uneducated
- Warmongers
- Boring
- Hypocrites

Every descriptive word they used is one you'd never want to be called; yet these words were being used to describe us. So the kid I'm talking with on the park bench asks, "If I become a Christian, do I have to be like that? Do I have to believe that homosexuals are going to hell? Do I have to be a Republican? Can I love science? Do I have to be . . . you know?"

Over the years I've mostly worked in fairly conservative

churches. And at times I've gotten the feeling that part of my job is not only getting kids into the faith but, more importantly, helping them grow up to be conservative. Conservative theologically, conservative morally, conservative politically . . . you get the idea. But I just have to ask, is this really my job? Is it my job to not only get students to Jesus, but also make sure they behave and believe what most evangelical Christians deem as being culturally acceptable? Do they have to be encouraged to vote correctly and to love apple pie and the American way? To take a strong stance for the inerrancy of Scripture and believe in the rapture? Really? *That's* in my job description? Just getting kids to open their lives to Jesus is more work than I can handle sometimes. Now I also have to make sure they believe in a literal six-day creation?

If it's true that the life stage of adolescence now lasts until a person is in his or her mid-twenties—and I believe that it's true—then we've got some time to work on those issues before our students reach adulthood. And honestly, I don't much care where they land on the nonessentials of life and faith. This young man who was sitting with me at the park just wanted to know if he could come to Jesus as is. He wanted to know if it was okay for him to come to God with his own thinking, his own ideas, bents, leanings, and understandings. I said, "Of course!"

Dr. Kenda Creasy Dean (pastor, author, and professor of youth, church and culture at Princeton Seminary) spoke to the upperclassmen in our youth group during a retreat. She was amazing and really challenged our students' thinking. Afterward, I was talking with one of our students who admitted that she felt so relieved. She said she'd been thinking about leaving the faith. She just wasn't sure if she could call herself a Christian any longer because her view of Scripture has changed. She told me her view of the Bible is that it's inspired by God, but that man's opinions are in there as well. She said that after listening and interacting with Kenda, she felt let off the hook a bit. Then she looked at me and said, "I just really want to follow Jesus and use my brain at the same time." I was proud of her willingness to stay engaged with her faith.

Now if you assumed that Kenda presented an "easy to follow" faith, you'd be wrong. She did present a gracious faith, yes. But she also challenged the MTD (Moralistic Therapeutic Deism) belief system (which I touched on in chapter one), and she challenged it in a big way. I was so impressed as she led our students away from religion and back to Jesus.

But in the midst of this post-Christian world, we have to allow space for students to explore and search and maybe even end up in a different theological paradigm than our own. This is not an easy task. Believe me, if I could just shake teenagers by the shoulders and yell at them to think what I think, I would do it. But this tactic is highly ineffective. (I've tried it with my wife, and she's not having any of it.) So what's the alternative?

EMBRACE CHRISTIAN RELATIVISM

I'd like to offer some food for thought, so please just hear me out. First of all, we have to begin by embracing what I've termed "Christian relativism."

"Whoa, Brock! What are you saying here?"

I know, I know. Just hold on a minute.

Years ago we did a series for our high school students called "Pick One." We took controversial issues in the Bible and taught all the different orthodox positions on the topic. For example, we taught on the topic of homosexuality. We looked at the Scriptures together, and then we talked about all of the different views and interpretations of those passages that are accepted by orthodox Christians. We also looked at hell, women in ministry, the end times, and many other issues.

The funny thing is—well maybe it's not so funny—this discussion brought a lot of heat my way. As you can imagine, both the church leaders and the parents wanted me to just tell the students *what* to think. However, I was more interested in teaching them *how* to think. I wanted them to know how gracious and big the faith was. I really don't care all that much if a student believes in the rapture or not.

So now back to that student who's chatting with me on the park bench. He's ultimately asking, "Is there room for all of me in this faith?" Embracing Christian relativism is, as Brian McLaren wrote in his brilliant book by the same name, a *generous orthodoxy.* What if Christians were seen as being generous? Generous with ideas, generous with theology, generous and patient and tolerant with each other and with the world. Another word for this would be gracious. What if Christians were known for showing grace to each other and the world, first and foremost? Right now the world looks at us and thinks, *Christians aren't even gracious toward each other. I hate to think what they might think of me!*

People need to know that the faith is big enough for them. That our orthodoxy is generous and allows for all kinds of positions on all kinds of issues. We need to remember to keep the main thing the main thing. Some things in the Christian faith are just relative. They are minor issues that can sometimes, mistakenly, take center stage. You can be a Christian, a follower of Jesus, and land in a different place on a host of topics and issues. It's what makes the faith so beautifully complex. And I believe the mystery of such things is a purposeful, sovereign act of God. We must show the world that we can disagree yet still love and respect each other.

To embrace Christian relativism is to embrace a unified faith. It's to embrace each other. Followers of Jesus must see the beauty in our diversity. To embrace Christian relativism is to actually live out Philippians 2. Check out verses one through four in *The Message*:

> *If you've gotten anything at all out of following Christ, if his love has made any difference in your life, if being in a community of the Spirit means anything to you, if you have a heart, if you care—then do me a favor: Agree with each other, love each other, be deep-spirited friends. Don't push your way to the front; don't sweet-talk your way to the top. Put yourself aside, and help others get ahead. Don't be obsessed with getting your own advantage. Forget yourselves long enough to lend a helping hand.*

Does agreeing with each other mean we agree on *everything*? I think not. It means we agree to love each other, to embrace each other, to honor each other's perspective. We must show students who are struggling in this post-Christian world what unity really is, what Christian relativism can look like, that we will cherish whatever they faithfully bring to the table as followers of Jesus. Now, I want you to know that I *am* aware of the danger here, but let me talk about that after my next point.

About a year ago I received an email from a parent telling me that her ninth grade daughter would no longer be coming to our youth group. The family doesn't attend church, although they consider themselves religious, and the parents felt their daughter's regular attendance at our church would end up confusing her. In the middle of her email, the mom basically said their family doesn't believe the things we believe. I wondered which of our beliefs would cause them to pull their daughter out of our group. So I called the mom and asked. Her response was that we probably didn't agree on hell, homosexuality, and other issues like that. I told her our group focuses on Jesus, and Christians hold to all kinds of positions on those issues. I also stressed to her that all are welcome in our church—but to no avail. We haven't seen that girl at youth group since. The perception that Christians are closed-minded and not welcoming was just too great for me to overcome in a phone conversation.

EMBRACE TOLERANCE

I realize the word *tolerance*, and maybe this whole chapter, might be setting off some warning sirens inside of you. But when did tolerance become our enemy? Don't get me wrong, I know what *tolerance* has come to mean in our culture. I just want to reclaim the word.

Tolerance doesn't write anyone off. True tolerance says you can belong *before* you believe. Tolerance embraces different thinking, differing views, and differing ideas—it embraces. What I find interesting is that the most tolerant students in our youth group are the ones who bring their friends most often. Why? Because they know how to tolerate their friends, and they also tolerate me as their youth leader. Our most tolerant kids are our best evangelists because they respect their friends' beliefs. At the same time, they are experiencing the transformative love of Jesus, and they want their friends to experience him too.

A student named Codey got involved with our youth group after he found the Lord at a summer camp. When he returned home, he told his aunt that he really needed to find a church. So they went looking for one and, fortunately for us, found ours. Codey has such a beautiful walk with Jesus, and he's one of the most thoughtful students I've ever met. When I first met Codey, his brother wasn't a Christian. And Codey doesn't have a single Christian friend at his school. Yet somehow Codey is a light, and his brother and friends all feel respected by him.

In fact, just last week Codey's brother went to camp with our youth group and surrendered his life to Jesus. It was amazing to watch the brothers embrace each other in a mutual love for Christ. I think one of the main reasons why Codey's brother invited Jesus into his life was because Codey has been consistently patient, kind, and respectful toward him.

Codey told me a friend of his has been getting into Buddhism, and he's really been learning a lot from this friend. Initially that kind of troubled me. But then I thought, *Why should this trouble me? I can't learn from a Buddhist?* Sure I can, and so can Codey. Here's the cool thing: he said his Buddhist friend encouraged him to start meditating, so Codey decided to look to Scripture to learn how to meditate. He's been meditating on the Psalms, and the Bible has truly been coming alive. Codey even thanked his friend for pointing him toward this spiritual discipline. Amazing! Tolerance not only accepts someone's view, but tolerant people allow themselves to be moved, to be pushed, and to be shaped.

All truth is God's truth, even if a Buddhist says it. So we don't need to cover up the fact that truth exists in other faiths and religions. Our students will realize it sooner rather than later, and we don't want them to be shocked when they hear a Muslim professor say something true. All truth is from God and belongs to him. And since we belong to God, all truth is ours.

What flies in the face of tolerance is this "Christian" notion that we have to be right all the time. For some reason Christians are willing to argue and fight, and we've earned a reputation for always needing to be right. Some Christians even refer to themselves as "the Christian Right." The need to always be right colors their interactions with everyone around them. I'd hate to think that people aren't open to Jesus because we're perceived as not being open to them. My prayer is that this reputation dies with my generation. It's creating a huge chasm between the post-Christian world and Christians that can't be crossed. Instead, the world needs to know that Christians are great listeners and great learners, that we are respectful and tolerant. Those traits are appealing.

I know we're getting into slippery-slope territory here. I can hear the questions already: "Brock, so far your first two points stink; they are ignorant and offensive. What are you thinking?! If we become Christian relativists and embrace tolerance, won't that lead kids to reject the faith? Doesn't that mean we're saying there's no absolute truth? Doesn't this devalue the authority of Scripture? Won't this lead to a free-for-all where people can believe anything they want to believe?" I hear you.

My first response is this: Post-Christian kids are already there. They're already rejecting the faith, they don't believe in absolute truth or the authority of Scripture, and they do believe whatever they want to. What I'm talking about is being tolerant toward students during their journeys, and then showing them how big our faith really is. It's not one-size-fits-all. Not only that, but we also need to show that there is unity in the faith, a commonality that every Christian, every denomination, and every church can point to. And that commonality is the Person of Jesus. What I'm really suggesting is that we embrace *humility*. Anything less than that is disingenuous. I mean, what if you're wrong about that one theological issue that you believe is so vital?

For many people, the church is a place that says, "If you don't believe what we believe, vote how we vote, and take the same stand on issues that we take a stand on, then you don't belong." I believe God is calling us to bigger things and a more humble posture. He is calling us once again to trust the Holy Spirit. To trust that he will work out the minor things of the faith in the lives of our students. When a kid lands on his or her view of homosexuality, Jesus won't fall off his throne. And who knows? Maybe over time the Holy Spirit will change a person's mind on that issue? Then again, maybe not.

I heard about a woman from India who became a Christian during the time of British rule. The British missionaries taught the female converts how Christian women dress and keep their homes. Many of the things they taught were actually healthier, cleaner, and seemingly better ways to live. The problem was that the Indian women started to act, behave, dress, and keep their homes in ways that alienated them from their native community. And rather than encompass these new converts into their own society, the British community acted in ways that were bigoted and demeaning toward them. Feeling isolated on both sides, these Indian women struggled to survive their ostracized existence. When the church ignores the realities that new believers face and refuses to embrace them as they are, we leave people feeling isolated and with no option but to return from whence they came.

Still feeling unsure? Consider what our choice to embrace tolerance is doing for the students at Trinity. They've gone from rejecting the faith to reading their Bibles, writing prayers, and making life choices that are pleasing to Jesus. And it's all because the environment of our group has allowed them to be themselves—whatever those selves might be at the time. They get to belong before they believe. And they get to belong as they wrestle with the details of those beliefs. They know they are safe in the church.

EMBRACE SPIRITUALITY

I've noticed a growing trend over the last few years. Some students in our youth group have been listing "spiritual" as their religious status on Facebook. Initially, this troubled me. I thought, *Are they ashamed to put "Christian"?* But as I said in chapter one, the word *Christian* has a negative connotation not only to Muslims, but also to post-Christian students. They might love Jesus, but they could never use the word *Christian*. It's a curse word. It comes with too much baggage.

However, they do resonate with the word *spiritual*. I had to come to terms with this one. I had to figure out why I struggled with the word *spiritual*. I mean, I have a spiritual life, and I think of myself as a spiritual person. But I felt like the word *spiritual*, as it's used in our culture anyway, was just too vague and uncommitted. (Like, pick a side, dude!) But in the context of a post-Christian world, I get it. And to be honest, I've become more and more uncomfortable with the word *Christian*. I don't like what *that* word has come to mean either. So I started thinking, *What if we helped students discover that the most spiritual life you can have is a life with*

Jesus? That knowing and following Jesus is the most spiritual way possible?

I was hanging out with Drew Williams, the lead pastor of our church (who is brilliant, by the way), when a student named Sam came over to chat with us. The three of us started talking and the conversation went to spiritual things. Sam said, "I'm one of the only religious kids in my class."

Drew corrected him and said, "Sam, you're not religious; you're spiritual. Religion is man-made; spirituality is from God."

Sam looked at him and said, "You're right; I'm spiritual." I kind of like that.

I know the term *spirituality* lacks a definitive definition. Social scientists have defined it as "the search for the sacred," where "the sacred" is broadly defined as "that which is set apart from the ordinary."[20] I love that definition. I want to be a person who is on a quest for things that are set apart. One of the reasons we struggle with the term is because it seems to separate itself from religion. But how many of us have told students that our faith is not a religion but a relationship? So again I pose this question: What if we could show our students who are living in this pluralistic society that following Jesus is the most "spiritual life" they could live? Let's reclaim that word and embrace it.

EMBRACE INTELLECTUALISM

I once heard an interview with Alec Baldwin during which the interviewer asked about his religion. Alec confessed that he goes to church every Sunday. When the interviewer asked him why, Alec responded, "Oh, because I love going and listening to professional thinkers." And I thought, *YES! Professional thinkers—that's how I want Christians to be seen.*

When I was in my late twenties, I started a habit of reading works written by agnostic, atheistic, or liberal-minded writers. I wanted to challenge myself a bit and get into the minds of people who don't believe in God because of their intellectual sensibilities. The first book I read floored me and sent me into a time when I doubted and questioned my own faith. But I figured if I couldn't handle these topics and work through serious questions, then I shouldn't be a youth pastor leading students into faith. I needed to wrestle a bit. It was important. One night at youth group, I was getting ready to walk out and explain the cross. It was a communion service, and I was preparing myself to point our students to Jesus in the clearest way possible. But I wasn't feeling very clear-minded; I was doubting and unsure. The worship band finished playing their last song, and I walked onto the stage in the midst of my doubts. I decided to stay faithful to what I was called to do as a pastor. I pointed them to Jesus. After that, I continued to wrestle and pursue truth, which brought depth to my shallowness. All truth is God's truth, and we can't be afraid of where truth might lead us. For me, it led me back to Jesus.

Socrates believed that intellectualism allowed a person to do what is right or best just as soon as they truly understood what is right or best. Understanding is critical for so many intellectual teenagers. If we don't embrace intelligent thinking and show students how sociology and science and psychology don't have to be at odds with the faith, then we are missing it. You can be a liberal-minded evolutionist and still follow Jesus. As Josh McDowell says, you don't have to check your brains at the door. If we don't embrace humble intellectualism, then we'll miss a whole barrage of post-Christian students.

Our students ask questions that I didn't *begin* to ask until I was in my twenties. While I was leading a small group of sixth grade boys, one said, "I'm agnostic; I don't really believe this stuff." This kid went on to talk about why he couldn't have faith because of what he believed about science. He'd watched something on the History Channel that talked about the earliest religions, prior to Christianity, and how they had a virgin birth messiah story as well. This kid's mind and his thoughts needed to be embraced, not disregarded.

A couple of years ago, a high school senior asked to meet with me to talk about the faith. She told me she just couldn't believe what I believed. I asked her why. She said science keeps her from faith. She longed to have faith like mine, but she just couldn't make the leap. I asked what her issues were exactly. She mentioned evolution. I told her to go ahead and believe in evolution; most Christians around the world are actually theistic evolutionists. She was surprised by this and felt relieved. She didn't want to abandon her faith, but she felt like society and the church were asking her to choose between faith and intellectual pursuit. God, in that moment, became so much bigger to her.

But keep this in mind: she didn't need me to show her that my way of thinking was wrong or that a conservative's way of thinking is reasonable—although there might be times when that is necessary. What she needed to see was that Christian faith is not at odds with her desire to learn and her respect for the natural world.

Modernists in the twentieth century loved to help Christians defend their faith. Liberal attacks in the early 1900s caused the Christian community to move to an insular, more defensive posture, which put us at odds with "the intellectual world." And at times we still use this language today. But intellectual honesty is so refreshing to our students. We have to become professional thinkers who join in and keep the beautiful questions alive. We must become the keepers of the questions, the ones to whom skeptics and thinkers are drawn.

EMBRACE MYSTERY

Intellectualism gets you only so far. As I embrace my mind and am open to the questions of others, I will come to a place where faith is required. All of my thinking and intellectual answers will come to an end, and this is where mystery begins. Reason and mystery give rise to each other as they act in relationship to one another giving us a depth we did not posses before.

We used to have quarterly "Doubt Nights" in our high school group. During the week before these evenings, students would write down their questions and their doubts about the faith. Then we'd pick a few and talk about them at the event. Our rule was that we didn't allow "pat answers." No easy answers to complex questions. But as the evening went on, we'd strategically lead students toward this idea of mystery, beautiful mystery. We'd share how God is so big and amazing and beyond us; that he is God and we are not. And every Doubt Night would end in exuberant worship. We'd worship the God who is above us and beyond our imaginations, who walks in front of our understanding. Honestly, students were never more engaged in worship than they were on these nights, and mystery got them there. Unanswered questions open us up to the bigness of God. When we offer pat answers to complex questions, we shrink God down to our level. We've gotten rid of all the mystery. Don't be afraid of mystery.

In a post-Christian world, mystery is acceptable. In fact, it draws students in. The modern world of the nineteenth century longed for answers to every question, but that's not the post-modern, post-Christian world we're living in today. Show students the mysteries of faith, and you'll find that they'll be drawn into worship.

EMBRACE THE MIRACULOUS

I went to a seminary that taught that miracles don't happen much today, that we live in a different dispensation of time in which God doesn't use miracles to get our attention, that the Holy Spirit just empowers people to be disciplined but doesn't do much else.

When we first arrived at Trinity Church, we were met with such opposition to the faith. The students didn't—they couldn't—believe in God. And especially not Jesus. So after about six months of building relational trust, I told them how I appreciated their doubts and their questions about the faith. But now I wanted them to do an experiment with me. I asked them to take their doubts and put them to the side for just a bit, for just a little while. And then I challenged them to open their lives to Jesus and see what would happen. I knew many of them were full of anxiety and needed God's peace. I suggested they ask God for it. I knew many of their families were really struggling. I asked them to invite Jesus into the middle of all of that. I was super nervous about doing this; but after studying what's been happening in Europe, I knew the post-Christian world is open to the miraculous. They long to see God move in real and true ways. If he is real, they want to experience him. So I prayed quietly, "God, you'd better come through here!"

Would you believe that God was getting ready to not only show himself to our students, but also increase my faith? God started answering prayers, students were coming to faith every week, and this little experiment of mine was working. And then we all went to camp. You'll never guess what happened next.

On the first night of camp, we began our worship time. Now you have to remember who I'm dealing with here. These students didn't know a single worship song, so projecting the lyrics was super important. Just as we began strumming our guitars, someone turned off the generator, and the light bulb in the projector went up in smoke. The projector was now dead, which meant the evening's program was going to be a bit more difficult to present. One of our students, who'd been experiencing God in prophetic ways, came to me and said he thought we should pray for the projector. I told him the bulb was broken and I'd tried everything I could think of to get the projector working again; it was impossible to fix. I clearly remember his response. He said, "Exactly." Basically, this tenth grade boy stood there and challenged me to have faith.

So we plugged my laptop into the projector and placed our hands on that stupid thing. I prayed these words, "God, it would be super cool if you could heal this projector." And then I added for good measure, "And we don't even need it on Friday night, Lord. Just get us through Thursday night's program." In a flash of light, the projector turned on and a verse from my keynote presentation on Acts 1 shone brightly on the wall:

> *"But you will receive power when the Holy Spirit comes on you; and you will be my witnesses in Jerusalem, and in all Judea and Samaria, and to the ends of the earth." (Acts 1:8, NIV)*

I was surprised, stunned, and I think a little pee came out.

But here's the really crazy thing: That projector worked *every* night of camp. Word got out amongst our group that God had healed our projector and that I'd prayed it would work through Thursday night. So then Thursday evening rolled around, the worship time came to a close, and I was praying with a student as the band strummed their last chord. Suddenly, the projector shut down. It just stopped working, and the light bulb was blackened and broken. Kids fell to their knees in wonder at the mystery of the God who not only heals anxiety and broken hearts, but also turns on small electrical appliances! He does so because he loves us and longs to be known by us.

I asked a European friend of mine what post-Christian Europeans are looking for spiritually. He simply said, "They are looking for a God who is alive and working, who answers their prayers and blows their minds." I thought, *Well, that sure sounds like the God I've been running into lately.* To be open to the miraculous doesn't mean you have to have pink hair and fake eyelashes, shake around the room, and preach health and wealth. You don't have to be weird. You can be intellectually sound, yet still believe that God is at work in miraculous ways. Maybe James meant what he wrote when he said, "You do not have because you do not ask God" (James 4:2, NIV).

EMBRACE ANSWERS

About 10 years ago, a bunch of post-modern youth ministry books hit Christian bookstores all over the country. These books taught that youth workers have to antagonize and challenge Christian thinking and instigate students to question their faith. At the time I completely agreed with their premise—and I still do in certain settings. But here's the danger: When your students are already asking critical questions because they're living in a culture that's antagonistic to the faith, then we must affirm faith when we see it.

Now, if little Tommy, a homeschooler who's been sheltered his whole life, offers a pat Christian answer to a very complex issue, then by all means challenge him! Make him uncomfortable and bring depth to his shallow faith. But if little Tommy is already struggling with faith because of his intellect, and he does verbalize faith, then affirm him. When he finds answers, encourage him and embrace his answers. I love that old saying, "Comfort the afflicted, and afflict the comfortable." I believe the same thing applies here: Affirm those who come to answers with difficulty, and challenge those who come to answers easily. We must know our audience.

Our mid-week program's teachings are based around the big questions of life. When a volunteer leader first joined our youth ministry team last year, he thought his job was to antagonize our students' answers—to question them and help them think critically. He grew up in a post-modern youth ministry program and just assumed this was the same approach we used today. But what he didn't realize was that our students have already worked through the criticisms of the faith. They have those down. They're post-Christian, after all. So what they really needed was for someone to help them see that their newfound faith is reasonable and makes sense. They need to know they're on the right track.

Every year we take our juniors and seniors on a "Theological Road Trip." Our goal is to help students land on the majors of the faith. We want them thinking theologically about everything. So this year we traveled to Princeton University, and, as I mentioned earlier, Dr. Kenda Creasy Dean was our keynote speaker. She stood in front of our students and just loved them. You could tell that, yes, she's a brilliant professor, but she's also a youth worker at heart. She really showed our students the bigness of our faith, that Christianity has a generous orthodoxy, that the faith makes sense, and that the answers they've been landing on are true. So many of our students are new to the faith, and we want to affirm this in them.

Youth ministry today is no easy task. You have to be a sociologist, a counselor, a pastor and a teacher, and an intellectual European charismatic. Ha! Tough stuff. And you have to do all of this in a world where it seems like everyone else is traveling on a freeway headed in the opposite direction—away from Jesus. But here's the truth: God has called you, and he actually believes in you. He knows that you and I can do this. And as we embrace this world with the kindness and love of Jesus, we will see students rise up and discover who they really are. What a gift. What a dream job!

CHAPTER FIVE

A NEW KIND OF MISSION

For the first 10 years of my life, I grew up on a tour bus. In the 1970s my parents were in a Christian rock band called The Amplified Version, and they traveled all over the country performing their hippie Jesus music. The cool thing was they truly had a heart to see teenagers come into a relationship with Jesus. But during this time, the church rejected their brand of music. In fact, kids would give their lives to Jesus inside the arenas while church people were outside burning the band's albums and protesting this "devil music."

I don't know if the church rejected them because the band sounded too contemporary or because their style of music wasn't folksy enough. But this antagonistic environment forced my parents' band to work outside of the church. Their bus would pull into a town on a Monday, and the band would find the highest place that overlooked the city. They would go to that spot and pray passionately that God would come and do an awesome work in the hearts, minds, and souls of every kid who lived there. Then they'd play at every high school and college all week long and invite kids to a Friday night concert. (Now this was during the Jesus Movement of the '60s and '70s, so Jesus was "just alright" with the youth culture back then.) Teenagers would come by the thousands, and hundreds

upon hundreds would give their lives to Christ. One of my
college professors told me he'd worked with Youth for Christ
in the 1970s, and he'd brought my parents' band to Chicago
with zero support from the churches. He also said it was one
of the most powerful weeks in his ministry there.

In the early '80s The Amplified Version disbanded, so to
speak. My parents became youth pastors and started discipling
students. As I watched them interact with teenagers, both
as members of the band and as youth workers, I remember
thinking they were radicals. They were living life with kids,
pointing them to Jesus in a world that was dead set against
the in-breaking kingdom. So when I got my own call to youth
ministry, I knew that if I ever worked in a church, it would
have to be outward facing and a blessing to its community.

Two weeks after we got married, Kelsey and I moved to
Southern California to minister in a town just outside of
Los Angeles. I was the middle school director at Glendale
Presbyterian Church, and I made all of $25,000 a year while
ministering to the five kids in the program. My boss at the
time was the brilliant Tim Galleher who served every week in
every high school in the city. I thought, *I'll do the same thing,
but I'll do it in middle schools.* One day I was talking with a
police officer, and I asked him who the most dangerous kids
in the city were. He told me they were middle school students
"because they are bored, they are trying to prove themselves
to the gang, and they have no sense of consequences."

So Tim and I had the idea to develop an after-school program
for middle school students in the city. I remember sitting in

front of the city council and asking for $100,000 to get it going. They gave me $80,000, and we were off and running. We offered an after-school boxing program, an after-school basketball program, and a teen pregnancy counseling center. And we also ran all of the school dances in the city. It was an exciting and grueling time of ministry, and overnight our little group of five middle schoolers became bigger than we could manage. Over the next 15 years, Kelsey and I worked in a couple of different churches in Southern California, discipling and equipping students while also trying to serve and be a blessing to the community.

When I first started doing youth ministry, I told students to be salt and light on their school campuses. I'd say things like, "Your school is the only mission field in the world that if you don't go to it, a truancy officer will come and drag you there." It was a difficult challenge 20 years ago for students to be a light at their schools. And as the years have gone by, this difficult missional hill has slowly become a mountain, a rugged and steep mountain. Students today find it nearly impossible to bring Jesus to school in this post-Christian world. And I soon found that it was an impossible ask on my part.

I've also grown weary of trying to disciple kids inside a youth room in just 90 minutes a week—especially since I know the only way they'll learn the way of Jesus is through on-the-job training. At the end of a typical night, I'd say to students, "Have a great week! See you next Wednesday." But as I started serving on school campuses, I loved saying, "See you at school tomorrow!" I would show students how to be salt and light at their schools by doing it myself. They could join me if they wanted.

In 2006, my family, along with ministry partners Peter and Katie Nelson, moved to the liberal Northwest to work in a church and start a nonprofit called The Common Good that would bless the schools in that region. My first order of business was to set up meetings with principals, teachers, and city officials to lay the groundwork for what an outward-faced youth ministry would look like. So there my team and I were, sitting in a coffee shop with a group of principals from this town in Oregon. It had taken a couple of months just to set up a meeting with them, but the day finally came. I explained what the mission of our nonprofit was and what we were trying to do. And then I asked, "What do you guys need? Is there any program or dream that you'd like to see happen if you just had the right amount of manpower, resources, or money?" Every principal said they were fine, thanked me for asking, and went on their way.

But a day later, one of the principals called me. He'd been a principal in that town for about 30 years. He was loved, and he was one of the most influential leaders in the city. He asked me if we'd be willing to help him with his school assemblies—apparently, they were awful. The teachers hated them, he hated them, and worst of all the students hated them. He said the school had no school spirit. So if we were willing, he'd love to have us take a shot at doing them. I was thrilled and told him we'd love to do it if he could give us about 30 of his finest students to pull it off. He gave us 60 student government kids.

We started meeting with them, dreaming, scheming, and putting together the best darn school assembly known to man. It went off without a hitch. We had kids flying in on zip lines, a freestyle contest, funny videos, and pie-in-the-face games. The best part was that I didn't get on the mic once; the students were the stars. Afterward, the principal asked if we could do that every month. So within two months, our role had grown into running the student government class on Monday, Wednesday, and Friday mornings. The student government kids would ask me, "Why are you here?" This is every minister of the gospel's dream question. I'd answer briefly, without proselytizing, and share about the call of God on my life in a fun yet vague kind of way. Some students were floored. Others said, "I *knew* there was something different about you." And still others confessed that they were followers of Jesus too.

Within another two months, we were responsible for all of the school's activities. We even started taking students to serve in a soup kitchen once a week. They'd just sign up to come with us during lunch period. As word got around to the other principals in the city, we started getting asked to do the same thing in their schools. One middle school needed mentorship help because 40 percent of their students didn't have a father living in the home. I asked how many mentors they needed, and they came back with a conservative 100. We partnered with some folks who felt called to this ministry, and they helped us by recruiting mentors from local churches, training them, and putting them in place.

Exciting things happened every week, and we really felt like we were a blessing to our community. The cool part is that instead of doing youth group dances or activities, our youth group kids participated in the public school's dances and activities. Our students ran the sound, worked as the DJ, operated the lights, set up, and tore down. And then they began dreaming about other ways they could be salt and light on their own campuses. We were able to break down the barriers between the sacred and the secular for our students, as we discipled young passionate activists who were developing kingdom values.

Once we'd shown ourselves to be committed, the principal who'd asked us to start with his school started feeling bad about getting something for nothing. "Brock, we kind of feel guilty. You're doing all of this work for us and not getting a penny. Is there anything you want to do?" I said we loved what we were doing. He said, "I know you're a youth pastor. Do you want to hand out flyers for your youth group?" I told him we would never do that. We weren't doing this to get more kids to come to our youth group. He prodded, "Come on, what would you like to do here if you could do anything?" What a question! I told him about my idea for teaching kids about social justice and connecting it to the history department. I said we could teach students all about the unjust things that are happening around the world, what people are doing to remedy those problems, and how students might get involved. He thought it was a brilliant idea and gave us the go-ahead.

Then he asked, "Anything else?" I told him that maybe as an all-school project over spring break, we could build houses for people in need of homes. He said, "You mean like a mission trip?"

I said, "Yeah, kind of like that."

His response? "Let's do it!"

God did amazing things in and through us. Instead of our church being insulated and inward, we started blessing our community. They were thankful we were there.

In order to be a blessing to our communities, we have to become more like and more *unlike* our culture. Tim Keller, senior pastor of Redeemer Presbyterian Church in New York City, said this during a webcast:

> *My understanding of how you reach a culture is Christians have to be extremely like the people around them, and yet at the same time extremely unlike them. If Christians are not unlike, they won't challenge the culture; but if they're not like, they won't persuade the culture. Now, hitting that middle ground is hard. Before the coming of Christ, believers were culturally different. Christ comes, and now you can be a Christian in every tongue, tribe, people, and nation. Jesus gets rid of the ceremonial laws and all those things that made Christians culturally strange. In that sense, [now] your neighbor is like you.*[21]

When we get out from behind the walls of the church and truly start caring for our community, we will become like our culture. We will care about what they care about, we will want the same things to succeed, and we will contribute to the whole. But when we don't promote our own stuff or ask for money or come with ulterior motives, then we are *unlike* the culture. We become a breath of fresh air. We become a blessing. That's when our youth ministry can become like what Jesus did with his disciples—on-the-job training. We get to live life with our students and show them what it means to be a blessing and live in the way of Jesus.

I spoke at the National Youth Workers Convention in 2012, and I talked about getting in the schools and serving. A hand went up in the back of the room and a young gentleman asked, "So are you seeing kids getting saved because you're in the schools?"

I don't think he, or many others in the room, liked my response. I said, "We don't serve to get people saved; we serve because we are saved." Ultimately, God saves people, and we are the fortunate ones who have the privilege of blessing them along the way.

At the end of their band years, my parents could no longer get inside the schools to sing. Too many Christians were preaching on school campuses and crossing the separation of church and state lines. They disregarded the rules and tried to evangelize the schools. Reaching a school is not about growing your youth group or increasing your salvation tally. It's about being Jesus with skin on. It's about living life well with your students right on their campuses and showing them how to serve others. And in the midst of doing this, we get to bless our communities in the name of Jesus.

But a major obstacle in doing this is that none of us have time to do much of anything in the schools. All of our time is spent running programs and youth events. About 20 years ago, a middle school boy came up to me at church and asked, "Hey, are you the activities director?" That's when I knew I needed to change what I was doing. I needed to stop entertaining and trying to attract students to my events. If we're honest, we'll admit that our "attractional" programs aren't attracting students nearly as well as they once did. We've got better sound, better lights, and unlimited quantities of pizza. But students today just don't care about those things.

I was talking with a fellow youth pastor who's looking to hire someone to focus on the high school ministry at his church. He said the church board had already thrown out some numerical expectations for this next hire. And their "BIG idea"? Pizza feeds. They said that when kids came to youth group en masse back in the early '90s, all the youth pastor needed to do was offer cool music and pizza. Sorry, those days are far behind us. I'm reminded of the book *Jim and Casper Go to Church.* In this incredible read there is an atheist, Casper, and a pastor, Jim, who travel around and attend services at many of America's "top" churches. After visiting all of them and experiencing the lights, cameras, music, and programs, Casper says to Jim, "Is this what Jesus told you guys to do?"[22]

So what if we made a change? You may have heard the term "sacred cows" used when referring to longtime programmatic expectations within the church. It's the attitude that we've always taken the students to *that* camp, or we've always met on *that* night of the week. Even though the surrounding culture has shifted, our ministry approach has not. We've accumulated so many programmatic "sacred cows" that we are ineffective to the point of impotence in a very different cultural time. We must kill the sacred cows—yes, the holy heifers must die! And then we've got to replace them with a more thoughtful and strategic approach. I love 1 Chronicles 12:32—*"from Issachar, men who understood the times and knew what [God's people] should do"* (NIV). We have to be like those men of Issachar.

But it's not just sacred cows that keep us from revolutionary ideas. Another major problem is that many of us work for lead pastors who served in youth ministry in the '80s and '90s. They can place upon us the mantle of loud music, big gatherings, and passionate speakers. But the culture has changed during the last 20 to 30 years. Youth culture today is about movement. So if we want to speak effectively to the rising generations, then our ministries must shift with the culture. This creates a conundrum for the lowly youth worker. Somehow we must lead those who are above us on the totem pole and also carry the vision to those around us.

April Diaz, human development director at Newsong Church in Irvine, California, just wrote an empowering book that I recommend you read. It's called *Redefining the Role of the Youth Worker*. In it, she outlines Bill Hybel's 360-degree leadership ideas and describes how she and her team at Newsong carried them out during a time of transformation in their church. See, you are in the position that you're in so you can lead not only those who are under you, but also your peers and your supervisors. You must carry the vision to the body of Christ.

But are we brave enough and in tune enough with the Spirit to know the way forward? In *Signs of Emergence: A Vision for Church That Is Always*, Kester Brewin wrote, "The perception of the new step will come only to those brave enough to stop dancing the old."[23]

As I've already mentioned, today's students are too busy, they are overscheduled, and the days when we could attract them to attend multiple youth activities in a week are long gone. But when we're entrenched in our communities and become a part of the social fabric of a school, that's how we can finally live life with our students. We'll be there coaching, teaching, and mentoring them in their world. If nothing else, we'll model what it means to be salt and light. So we need to cut back on our programs and leave space for living. We must give away our resources. Youth pastors who do this will move away from being folks who just sit in a room and talk to students about being light, and they'll become living, breathing lights in this dark world.

But first we have to get down on our knees and ask God to give us a revolutionary vision. I pray that we would contextualize our own communities and bring radical change to our ministries within an increasingly post-Christian culture. I love the vision of President Dwight Eisenhower's parents. Donald Miller explains it this way:

> *Eisenhower was a character, getting himself kicked out of West Point, causing a lot of trouble. But always there was in him a sense of confidence, a sense that he would become somebody important. And more than this, he believed the world needed him—that if he didn't exist, things would fall apart. He believed he was called to be a great man. I wondered, as I read, where he got this confidence, and that's when Eisenhower started talking about his family... he said his mother and father made an assumption that set the course of his life—that the world could be fixed of its problems if every child understood the necessity of their existence... If you believe your family will fall apart without you, you probably go on to believe your community will fall apart without you, and then your city and country. And in just about every dynamic you walk into, you would feel the need to lead, to hold things together, to bring life and service to the people you interact with—just as you had done when you were a kid with your family.*[24]

Your community *needs* you to struggle for them. And it may begin with you filling out a volunteer form in the school office. Our kids live at their schools, and they need us to get down off the stage and go where they are. This fall our youth group plans to launch an outward-facing missional ministry in our community, and God is already opening doors for us. If we can get inside the schools in Greenwich, Connecticut, and begin serving people, then you can do it anywhere.

Last night my wife and I went to the highest point of our town to pray over our community like we always do. We passionately asked God to do an awesome work in the hearts, minds, and souls of every kid who lives in this city. We asked that God would give us favor as we try to bless the people who live and work there. We prayed for revival.

CHAPTER SIX

CREATING AN ENVIRONMENT OF GRACE

We have an amazing volunteer leader named Josiah on our team. He's in his early twenties, and he constantly runs after students, caring for them, taking them out to eat, going rock climbing and skateboarding with them. And he's doing all of this because he feels called to it. It's like God handpicked him to pour his life into our students. But when I first asked Josiah to be a youth leader, he was really hesitant. He thought he'd be a terrible leader, and he even told me about a time when he was a junior in high school. Back then he was smoking pot regularly, and his youth pastor learned about it right before the youth group's mission trip. So the youth pastor told Josiah he couldn't come on the trip. I had to laugh, thinking, *If we didn't allow kids who smoke pot to go on our mission trips, then practically no one would be allowed to go.*

I resolved to keep pursuing him. I knew he loved Jesus, and I could tell he'd be great with our students. But that feeling inside of him—of being disqualified—was robbing him of his calling. Josiah hadn't gotten over getting kicked off that mission trip. It was still hanging over him, and he needed to be freed from the power of that event from his past. He needed grace.

Sometimes in the middle of a ministry event, students will discover something that somehow changes everything. Sometimes they'll get a glimpse of who they really are, and it astonishes them. When I was in middle school, I started going to camps with the youth group in my church. Initially, I went for three reasons: the girls, my friends, and the girls. What would happen—and this happened almost every time—is somehow I would live differently in those places: up in the mountains, by the beach, on a houseboat, wherever the camp happened to be. I would live life with people who loved God, loved me, and accepted me. By the end of camp, I would begin to see life in a different way. Although I rarely went looking for Jesus, he would consistently show up and give me just a glimpse. He would surprise me. Those trips slowly changed me. And even though I managed to show up for the next trip having reassembled every negative thought and attitude that I'd rejected during the last trip, I never felt like God was disappointed in me.

A student named Mark graduated from our youth group about three years ago. One year we took Mark and some of our other students on a mission trip to the inner city of San Francisco. When we pulled into the neighborhood where we'd be staying, the Tenderloin district, our students didn't want to get out of the vans. They were terrified! We could see about 200 homeless people hanging out, sleeping, smoking, and taking part in "extracurricular" activities. Just outside my van door was a woman smoking a crack pipe. When I saw my students' expressions, I thought, *This is going to be an amazing week!*

Now, back to Mark. At that time in his life, Mark was an amazing young man in the midst of a rough journey. About three months before our trip, he was taking part in all the wrong things—the kinds of things my youth pastor used to warn us against when he'd say, "Don't smoke, drink, or chew, or go with people who do." Well, Mark did all of that and more. In fact, just prior to our trip, he'd smoked pot with his mom. Now, I can imagine doing a lot of things. I can even imagine smoking pot. But not with my mother! Mark's home life was, to say the least, dysfunctional. And he was kind of a broken mess.

But on this mission trip, Mark began the transformation of his life. It started with simple living. Living life with and serving others for almost two weeks began to change him. Adult leaders, saw something in him that he couldn't see in himself, and pointed him to Jesus by the way they lived. Needless to say, Mark thrived in this environment. I believe we all would thrive in similar circumstances because that's how life is supposed to be lived.

All week we talked about how God is a runner and he is running after the hurting, the broken, the addicted, and the helpless. And he is calling us to run with him, which is pretty amazing. He wants us to bring change to places that desperately need change. We focused on this Scripture passage:

You've all been to the stadium and seen the athletes race. Everyone runs; one wins. Run to win. All good athletes train hard. They do it for a gold medal that tarnishes and fades. You're after one that's gold eternally.

I don't know about you, but I'm running hard for the finish line. I'm giving it everything I've got. No sloppy living for me! I'm staying alert and in top condition. I'm not going to get caught napping, telling everyone else all about it and then missing out myself. (1 Corinthians 9:24-27, The Message)

For the whole week, we preached on this passage about running after God and others. And all the while Mark was thinking, *No way! I'm too screwed up for God to run after me, to use me, to ask me to run with him to help others.* But God kept pursuing Mark in little ways. Mark listened to the talks all week, took part in the discussions, read the Bible for himself, and served the hurting people in the inner city. His eyes were being opened to how amazing God is and how God wanted to free him from his past and give him hope and a future. Toward the end of the trip, Mark started feeling like maybe he was meant for something more than getting wasted on the weekends. Maybe God really *did* want to change his story and use him to help others.

One night our group took a break from serving. We got some ice cream and hung out in a park overlooking the Golden Gate Bridge. The sun was setting, a cool breeze was blowing off of the Bay, and we were laughing together. Then in the middle of all this fun, our worship leader started strumming his guitar and singing prayers to Jesus. The students gathered around him, and a spontaneous time of worship broke out. I just sat there feeling amazed by what God was doing in our students' hearts. After about 15 minutes, there was a lull in the worship time. The guitar music still softly played in the background, and we all stood in the quiet.

Suddenly, a voice rang out from the darkness, "My name is Mark, and I'm a runner!" I was shocked—Mark was discovering who he really was. He was learning that he's not defined by his failures, his hurt, his family dysfunction, or his sin. He is a runner and he is running after God. His declaration began a chain reaction as the other students started yelling at the top of their lungs, "My name is _____, and I'm a runner!" Kid after kid joined this prayer anthem. I knew I'd just witnessed a miracle. Our students, through Mark's lead, were declaring truth to themselves and to anyone within earshot: God wasn't just running after the homeless; he was running after *them*. God wanted us to know that he created us to be a reflection of him—runners in this life.

We weren't looking for God that night; we just wanted to hang out. But he was still there. He was with us. Have you ever been doing the mundane or the ordinary when it suddenly becomes a sacred moment? In those moments we get a glimpse of how life is supposed to be lived.

The essence of youth ministry is to create environments where students can experience the warmth of God. With every talk we give, every game or activity we lead, and every time we run into students at the mall, they experience God's warmth. And that's because our relationship with Jesus is our ministry. We get to demonstrate that God not only loves students, but he actually *likes* them. We are the vehicles through which God shows students his overwhelming and amazing grace. He wants them to know that he delights in them, that he sings and rejoices over them just because of who they are right now (Zephaniah 3:17). That's grace.

The word *grace* can mean many things. We refer to a ballet dancer as having grace. We say grace before meals. We talk about the Queen of England carrying herself with elegance, refinement, and grace. But most importantly, *grace* means unmerited favor. It means giving special favor to someone who doesn't deserve it, who hasn't earned it, and who can never repay it. What if we saw our students as the favored ones? The ones to whom God has chosen to display his amazing grace?

GRACE IS UNFAIR

I love the parable of the prodigal son. In that story the son returns home after destroying his father's reputation, spending all of his inheritance, and falling into debauchery. The son expects to be punished and thinks the best-case scenario is if his father takes him back as one of his servants. But that's not the way grace works. Grace doesn't look for things that have been done that deserve love. Grace operates apart from the right behavior or the ability of the individual. Grace is one-sided; grace is God-sided.

I would have loved to see the son's expression when his father embraced him, kissed him, and then responded in a ridiculously extravagant way to his lost son's arrival. He placed a signet ring on his son's finger and dressed him in royal clothing. The son had feared, and rightly so, that his father would be like other fathers. And our students have that same fear about us; they fear that we'll respond or act like the other adults in their lives. But we're supposed to show them grace—God's grace. Unfortunately, they probably don't see God quite the same way that Jesus paints him in this parable. Can you imagine the prodigal son's shock? He wasn't going to spend the rest of his life working as his father's slave. No, he received a whole new beginning! He was lifted up before the community and publicly celebrated. Expecting a judgment or discipline, instead he received grace and words of affirmation.

But we all know this story. We've taught it. We've even experienced it. But man is it hard to live out. Just now as I'm writing this, I feel convicted. I feel like I owe an apology to a student in my youth group. She won't expect it; in fact she kind of wronged me. She had a bad attitude about something a couple of months ago, and she tried to make a power play, backing me into a corner to get me to change something. I even conceded a bit, but then I drew the line in the sand and responded with, "Hey, I'll give you this, but you can't have it all!" I was kind of short with her, and it really wasn't a big deal. But inside, I knew I wasn't showing her grace. I felt a little offended by how she acted, and it showed in my response to her. It was a tense moment between us for sure. Yet I've never spoken about it, never apologized for my part in it, and I haven't cleared the air. Right now I'm convinced that I need to go to her and say I'm sorry. I want to lavishly dump grace all over her. She is the favored one.

In a post-Christian world, we'll run into all kinds of students. Students who are angry, who doubt, who are hurting and addicted. We'll run into students who are led by their emotions, who are stressed-out, who have the weight of the world on their shoulders, whose families are messy, and who have believed cultural lies. In the midst of this pluralistic world, all of these students are trying to figure out who they are. They definitely don't need to feel like they must try to live up to one more adult's expectations. We should create an atmosphere where students feel free to express who they are in the moment and what they believe this afternoon—even if it's all going to be different tomorrow. In the midst of the adolescent roller coaster ride, the grace we give them might be one of the only places where they'll find it.

GRACE HAS A LONG-TERM VISION

Our goal should not be helping 15-year-olds become godly. Our goal should be that one day when these 15-year-olds are 30-year-olds, their faith will influence who they marry, what careers they choose, what habits they form, and how they raise their children. And grace is a slow teacher. Titus 2:12 says, *"[Grace] teaches us to say 'No' to ungodliness and worldly passions, and to live self-controlled, upright and godly lives in this present age"* (NIV). Grace teaches us to say no to using passive-aggressive manipulation, discipline, and timeouts, or to kicking kids off mission trips. Beautiful, amazing grace. And grace teaches us over and over again. When we mess up, God's grace beats judgment to the punch every time. In that moment of failure, we are introduced to God's relentless nature. God's grace never stops short, never runs out, and never dries up. No matter how many times I blow it. No matter how many times I go back to the same old me with the same old junk, grace just keeps teaching; it keeps showing up. Grace keeps pointing me to the radical love of God. That's what's changing me, and it will change our kids too.

GRACE CREATES SPACE FOR FAILURE

When failure occurs, grace enters the room. Our ministries must be spaces where kids can make mistakes, lose their tempers, royally mess up. In order to create an environment of grace, you must first create an environment where authenticity is valued and failures are lovingly tended. Then grace gets to do what grace does. If we are creating an environment of moralism, where kids feel the need to put on their "Christian" selves before they walk through the door or put their best selves on display, then we'll never see what's going on beneath the surface. If there are no failings, then there is no place for grace and patient restoration. There's no need for it.

I love Luke chapter 7. Jesus seems to be saying that he likes it when people sin greatly, so they can be forgiven greatly. It's like cleaning a bathroom—it's gratifying in the end because it was so disgustingly dirty to begin with. The transformation is glorious and draws praise for the one who did the work to clean it. Jesus sees our sin as an opportunity to show off just how big his grace is. (I know I'm bordering on heresy here, but what else is new?) Read it for yourself:

Now when the Pharisee who had invited Him saw this, he spoke to himself, saying, "This Man, if He were a prophet, would know who and what manner of woman this is who is touching Him, for she is a sinner."

And Jesus answered and said to him, "Simon, I have something to say to you."

So he said, "Teacher, say it."

"There was a certain creditor who had two debtors. One owed five hundred denarii, and the other fifty. And when they had nothing with which to repay, he freely forgave them both. Tell Me, therefore, which of them will love him more?"

Simon answered and said, "I suppose the one whom he forgave more."

And He said to him, "You have rightly judged." (Luke 7:39-44, NKJV)

In a post-Christian world there is some pretty good sinning going on. So I instruct our youth ministry leaders to look for the distracted, the distracting, the angry, the doubting, and the hungover students each week. It's an opportunity to get with those students and find out what's going on. We see it as God's cue to extend grace to them. The Holy Spirit makes us aware so we can show up and dump love all over them. Grace surely loves us as we are, but it never leaves us as we are. God loves us too much for that.

During a time of sharing, we asked our students to express what they love about the youth group. The overwhelming response was that they felt like they could authentically be themselves. They felt loved and more alive when they experienced God together.

In the beginning of this book, I told you about John, my tenth grade friend who heard God tell him that reincarnation is true. His story continues when, about a year later, he called me up in a panic and asked if I'd meet with him as soon as possible. Within 10 minutes he was sitting on my back porch, sipping a soda, and unloading on me all of the uncomfortable details about what he'd done at a party the night before. He spared nothing. Then he asked, "Will God forgive me or will he reject me?"

I looked at him and said, "Well, he won't reject you, but he is really disappointed."

Just kidding. I actually bragged about my Jesus. I told John all of the wonderful details of God's unmerited favor. Symbolically, I put a signet ring on his finger and dressed him in royal clothing. I had the privilege of declaring that perhaps the Good News is better news than we ever dreamed of. Grace.

CHAPTER SEVEN

A NEW MEASUREMENT FOR SUCCESS

It's springtime. The flowers are blooming, the rains come in every couple of days to wash everything clean, and the sun is warming us up. I just love this time of the year. But I also hate it. Springtime seems to be when churches decide to fire their youth workers. I guess they figure the spring mission trip is over, the school year is wrapping up, and they need to hire a new youth leader so that person can get used to the job before the busy fall semester begins. Three youth worker friends of mine were fired in the last two weeks. But it's not just in the spring that I've seen this happen. In fact, I've been hearing about youth workers getting fired en masse over the last five to ten years. In all my years in youth ministry, I've never seen so much firing, and it makes me angry.

I had a conversation with a lead pastor about this issue, and he said he thought more youth pastors are getting fired because this generation of youth workers doesn't know how to work hard. He said, "They're lazy and they can't draw a crowd." Then he went on to say something to the effect that youth workers today can't seem to do what he and his friends were able to do with previous generations of students. I told him he was an idiot.

Over the last 30 years, church work has become more professionalized, leading many churches to hire businessmen to implement business strategies in the church. While this change has helped the church on many fronts, such as fiscal integrity, it has also turned parishioners into clients, pastors into salesmen, and the gospel into a product. A while back I was in a meeting where an executive pastor started talking about how churches must have quantifiable and measurable goals. Now I'm all for having measurable goals (and we'll talk about this some more later on in the chapter), but it's very difficult to measure anything other than numbers. And once we've collected the numbers, we can't help but compare them to the numbers from previous years or to other churches' numbers.

A brilliant youth worker friend of mine called to tell me he was quitting youth ministry. He said he didn't want to carry the weight of the church's ridiculous expectations any longer. He was tired of having a constant pit in his stomach, and he didn't like what the church was turning him into. Doesn't that sound odd coming from someone who works in Jesus' church? God forgive us!

A church asked me to do some consulting and help them find their next youth pastor. I asked if I could speak with their previous youth pastor first. They initially said they didn't think that would be a good idea. Hmm? But I pressed it and they eventually caved and let me speak to her. It's never a good sign if an organization, especially a church, won't let you speak with their previous employees. So I spoke with this woman on the phone; and as we began to talk, I quickly realized that she was broken by her experience at this church.

There were long periods of silence because she was weeping and couldn't answer my questions. I spent the better portion of an hour just ministering to her and trying to repair some of the damage this church had caused.

I can empathize. Yes, I've worked in healthy church environments, but I've also ministered in unhealthy ones. I've endured plenty of sleepless nights and even a few stress-induced panic attacks over some difficult situations at the church. I've worked in an environment where the ministry took precedence over the minister, where the head count was considered a priority over heart change. We can try to spiritualize the numbers, but that approach can easily be misused. And it creates a "cog in the machine" environment for pastors. Running the race to beat last week's/month's/year's numbers is exhausting and a no-win situation.

There is a crisis in American churches today: youth workers have become disposable pieces in the machinery of the church. It chews them up, leaving them damaged and traumatized. And this trend is on the rise because churches still expect large crowds of students to gather weekly, even in this progressively post-Christian environment. The world is changing, but the church's expectations haven't adjusted to the climate in youth culture today. The leaders in many of our churches use pressure tactics to try to get the results they want. It creates a stifling context to minister in for sure.

Let me say something here about job evaluations—just in case a lead pastor or a future lead pastor is reading this book. Most performance reviews begin with the boss telling you a few positives, and then they drop the bomb by naming all of the things you still need to work on or improve. Such a list essentially negates all of the positive things they just said about you. And there usually isn't much constructive criticism or anything concerning your personal well-being either. It's just a list of your "shortcomings" based on the church's vision of what student participation should look like. You know what I'm talking about. Well, today I had my year-end review with the lead pastor of our church. And my boss handed me a document that may have been the most thoughtful and insightful review of my work and the ministry that I've ever seen. He began with 14 paragraphs detailing all of the wonderful things he's been seeing. And then he dropped the bomb. The list of things I need to work on. Want to know what was on the list? *Rest*. That's it. Pretty cool, huh?

He wants me to rest more, to feed my soul. He knows my pastoral heart keeps me up at night over the lives of teens. He actually pays attention to the fact that I frequently don't get my Fridays, or any day, off each week. When there is a calendar meeting for all of the pastoral staff, his mouth drops open when he hears about the amount of time and energy my little team and I spend running after students and creating environments in which they'll sense God's warmth. He is aware that I spend hours every day counseling students and parents, and that when I go to a retreat or camp, it's not a vacation for me.

So I'm taking the next six months off to rest . . . I wish!

Seriously, though, I want to work hard for a boss like that.

There are some people you want to work for, for the rest of your life. And I'm so blessed to work for one of those guys.

We've already talked about why youth ministries around the country are numerically in decline. Culturally we are fighting an uphill battle. But in order to understand this issue further, you've got to get into the mind of a Christian teenager. Now imagine that you're a 16-year-old in your church's youth group. As Chap Clark described in his book *Hurt*, you have multiple authentic personalities. You have your church self, your home self, and multiple selves at school depending on which class you're in and who you're with. You might have a different self in English class than you do in history. And you consider all of these selves to be your authentic self in each of those environments. You just put on the "you" that feels safest in that environment.

Let's hypothesize that your church/spiritual self only feels comfortable with loving Jesus, praying out loud, and growing spiritually at youth group meetings or church. Let's also say that the youth pastor is asking you to invite friends from school to a youth group event. Church self doesn't want your school friends to come to youth group because that's the only place where your spiritual self can shine. You feel safe there when you're away from your school friends. And you don't want the youth group to grow. Or if it does grow, you want kids you don't know to come so that your church self can continue to feel safe. But the youth pastor is trying to keep her job. She's trying to keep the church board happy by doing whatever she can to grow the group numerically. Yet none of the students are willing to help her do this. In fact, the idea of the group growing bigger scares them. They like it the size it is now. They want it to stay the same. That's one of many dilemmas youth workers face today.

Twenty years ago if I told high school students to invite friends to special events, it would double or triple the amount of students at youth group that night. Today, students don't want their school friends to see them at youth group.

It's like the *Seinfeld* episode where George's worlds start to collide because Jerry, Elaine, and Kramer start hanging out with his fiancé Susan. George doesn't want Susan interacting with his friends, and he definitely doesn't want them to become friends. He doesn't want to lose the sense of safety that keeping different aspects of his life separate provides. Why? "Because a George divided against himself cannot stand!" Students have multiple selves and multiple worlds. They don't want their worlds to collide.

In the youth ministry world of the 1980s and 1990s, numbers determined success; they were the driving force of youth work. We even spiritualized numbers by calling them "souls." Don't get me wrong, numbers are indicators, and they're important ones at that. But there are other ways to determine success in a post-Christian world—more valid ways.

INDIVIDUAL CARE

The first marker for a successful youth ministry is individual care. Does every student in your church have caring adults assigned to him or her? This has got to be our priority. Every student, no matter how he or she appears on the outside, is desperate for a dedicated fan, a loving adult to come alongside and journey through life with them. I just asked some of our tenth grade girls what the best thing about the youth group is. (I was expecting to hear things like my talks, our programs, or our mission trips.) The first thing they said was, "The adult volunteers." They absolutely love their small group leaders! They feel heard, cared for, known, and respected.

When a kid misses youth group, we know why. We know what's going on. When a kid misses two months of youth group because of play rehearsals at school and then shows up again after such a long time away, we don't say, "Hey, where have you been?" We know where she's been because her small group leader is a part of her life. Even though she couldn't make it to youth group, she's still been getting together with her leader for coffee after rehearsals each week.

Youth leaders should be kids' dedicated fans. Every kid must feel cared for and pursued, and every student has to know that we want to spend time with them—and not just at "our" events. This is going to require a huge cultural shift in our churches. Members of the congregation must change from being supporters of the youth to seeing these students as their students. You've read the books. You know students need about four dedicated adults in their lives. The church must wake up to this need; otherwise we'll continue losing the students we claim to love and care about. But we'll talk about that in just a minute.

TOUCHPOINTS

Success in youth ministry shouldn't be based on student attendance. Instead, a second indicator for success might be called touchpoints. How many times have we reached out to students this month? It's not about how often they come to our meetings; it's how often adult leaders have gone to their activities. How many texts or Facebook messages have they received from us? Or how many coffeehouse meetings have we invited them to? Have we reached out to them? These are called touchpoints.

There's a student who's been to our youth group only a couple of times this year. He's been gone from one season to the next, beginning with cross country, SAT testing, play rehearsals, and then the golf team. But his group leader has personally spent time with him on many occasions. He's met with this student for coffee, watched his sporting events, and texted him regularly. When our students are involved at their schools, which is what we want, then we have an opportunity to do what Jim Rayburn called *incarnational ministry*. God became one of us in the person of Jesus. He came to where we were. It's time for us to get out of the youth room.

INTEGRATION WITH THE CONGREGATION

Third, we can determine the success of our ministry based on how we're doing at assimilating students into the church body. How integrated are your students with the rest of the congregation? This is a tough one. The structures and programs of many of our churches aren't sensitive to the fact that 15-year-olds are in the room. Case in point: we call the main service "big church." This has got to end. We can spearhead this change and advocate for our students to be included. In order to do this, the next step of integration will help us immensely.

My great-grandmother was the youth worker at her church in Oregon from the 1930s through the 1960s. She actually led my grandmother, her future daughter-in-law, to the Lord when my grandmother was just 12 years old. All of the students sat with her in the front row every Sunday morning during the church service. They absolutely loved her. She was constantly including the students in the life of the church. This was the norm for the church back then. It was generational, and kids saw themselves as part of a multigenerational group of people called to be salt and light in their community.

Hinging on the success of groups like Young Life and Youth for Christ in the 1970s and into the 1980s, churches started hiring youth directors for the first time. They abandoned an integrated form of church life and pulled students out of the church body. They hired youth workers to run completely separate programs, retreats, missions, and services away from the church family. So what once was a group of teenagers fully integrated into the life of the church now became a youth ministry ghetto. No longer did students see their identities as being a part of the church family. Over the years this has become the norm in churches around the country, so when kids graduated from high school in the late 1980s through the present, they also left the church. Hiring a 22-year-old and paying that person an extremely low amount of money to disciple students apart from the church has an effect. Many students graduate from the youth group and simultaneously graduate from their faith.

Integration is key. Integration means we shut down the youth ministry ghetto. Integration means we put pathways back in place. It is vital that students see the generations ahead of them loving and serving Jesus—people become pathways for students. Teenagers have to be able to envision themselves as a part of the church when they're older. And we help them do this by allowing students to serve and worship with adults who are including them in the life of the church. You won't be able to do this overnight, but we have to carry the vision to others.

An integrated youth ministry means we stop doing a guys retreat and we join the church's men's retreat. It means we get students involved in leading in the main service. We give them a role and we see them as a valuable part of the church family. The system of the church must change, and we must adapt in order to receive the next generation. In order for kids to make it in the post-Christian world, they need a bunch of adults around them who see them as a part of the church family. Our job as youth workers is to lead a movement, a movement of adults who invest in this new generation. We get the privilege of carrying this vision of integration and inclusion. That means we're always training and encouraging our adults to love students better.

So what would happen if we disbanded the youth ministry ghetto? What if we stopped running alternate programs separate from the church? What would that free us up to do? What if we integrated our mission trips and our retreats with other ministries in the church? How much freedom would that give us? I know it would create some problems, but we already have massive problems and obstacles to overcome. What solutions might this change bring? And what if students began getting their identities from being a part of the church rather than being apart from the church?

REACH OUT TO THE PARENTS

Fourth, much of a student's success is based on his or her home environment. In fact, the National Study of Youth and Religion found that students directly inherit their parents' faith. So if a kid's default religion is Moralistic Therapeutic Deism, then guess what? That means their parents have given this religious construct to them. We have to reach mom and dad.

When I was 23 years old, I ran my first parent meeting. About five really good parents showed up, and I spoke to them for about an hour and a half. I talked about what was going on in our youth ministry, but then I began telling them how I thought they should be parenting their kids. After the meeting a very nice, but blunt, mom came up to me and said, "Brock, you don't know what the hell you're talking about!" Ouch! She was right; I was clueless.

I'm in my 40s now, and I've learned some things. This is key, by the way. Many youth workers get out of youth ministry before they have the wisdom and experience to help parents. Some of the best youth ministries in the country are run by youth workers in their forties and fifties. And that's because they finally have enough real-world experience to help the parents. I have a voice in the lives of teenagers because they know I care about them; however, I also have enough life experience that I now have something to offer their parents.

If you're a young youth pastor, you can still develop a year-round program that will help train and encourage the parents in your ministry. You can bring in guest speakers, plan retreats, and hand out resources. But if it's true that students grow up and inherit the habits and the faith of their parents, then we must do something to acknowledge and support them.

PRAY

The next way we can measure success is with prayer. I once heard Francis Chan speak at the National Youth Workers Convention. He got up in front of a few thousand youth workers and said, "When I'm looking for a youth pastor, I'm not looking for someone who is cool and hip to youth culture. I just want someone who will pray over our students." We all sat in silence. I was cut to the quick. I felt convicted. I sensed a calling back to Jesus. And it's true: I *can't* change anyone with my cool youth talks. I can't change a student's heart, but God can. I can't even change my own daughter's heart, but God can.

What I've found is that prayer works. Will someone pray for my daughter? Will someone pray for every student in my church? Will someone join me in bringing our students before the throne of God? This is what I look for whenever I hire someone or when we're looking for youth ministry volunteers. So how much are you praying? This is a vital measure for success.

Think about it: your boss calls you into his office and asks, "How are things going in the youth ministry?"

And you say, "We've got 20 people praying for our students every day, and we're seeing God work because of it." Success!

STORIES OF TRANSFORMATION

Lastly, we can measure our success by stories. In particular, stories of transformation. What is God doing? How is he working? What prayers is he answering? When we have a great event and more than the usual number of students show up, I don't go around the office or stand in front of the church and tell them how many students came. If I did that, then I'd be telling everyone that I measure success by the numbers. Instead, I tell stories to anyone who will listen: to the administrative assistants, maintenance workers, fellow pastors, moms, and my neighbors. I tell anyone who will listen. And then I invite them to pray for the students in those stories.

I make the rounds at least a couple of times a month. I just walk around the office and carry the vision of our students to my coworkers. I tell them about students like Evan and Freddie and Harry. I tell them about Ruth and Krista and Zoe and Jenny. I tell them what God is doing in their lives. This habit of mine has caused people to no longer ask, "So how many kids did you have last night?" Instead they ask, "So what did God do?" Then I get to brag about my Jesus.

Success is a funny word in the context of ministry. Somehow it has come to mean large not deep, loud not still, and entertaining not equipping. I love Mike Yaconelli's legendary talk about getting fired for the glory of God. And I'm baffled by the fact that Jesus would probably get fired from many of today's churches. According to the religious leaders of his day, Jesus said the wrong things, did the wrong things, and reached the wrong people; and eventually, the crowds died down. He even looked at the Twelve and asked, "You do not want to leave too, do you?" (John 6:67, NIV).

As ministers of the gospel, let's be the standard-bearers. It's our mission to carry a new vision of caring for students and loving them through this tough terrain called life. The church today might never be kind to this generation of youth workers. Like the prophets of old, we might get stoned (and I don't mean on pot). So let's travel lightly, love deeply, forgive quickly, pray often and pray desperately, speak truth, and, like the prophets, be ready to move.

CHAPTER EIGHT

KEEP SINGING

I've consistently found myself burning the wick at both ends. It's a problem that many of us in ministry struggle with on a regular basis. Overcommitted, rushing around, planning like crazy people with zero time for our souls. I heard Anne Lamott speak at a Youth Specialties pastors' convention one year. She looked around the room full of a few thousand pastors and said, "Do you want to know why we don't come to you pastors anymore? It's because you're just like us, burning the wick at both ends. You haven't heard from God in years." I was floored. And then I went home and changed absolutely nothing about my life.

The next year when I attended the National Youth Workers Convention, I heard a similar message shared by one of my youth ministry heroes, Mike Yaconelli. He spoke passionately about rest and how Jesus is longing for us to live in the presence of his amazing peace. Again, I was deeply convicted to go home and do nothing about it. I just kept up the pace that was drowning out the voice of Jesus in my life.

A few weeks ago I had an amazing conversation with another youth worker. He shared how burdened he feels over the students in his church. It felt so good to hear someone verbalize what I feel on a regular basis. We listened to each other, shared our hearts, and then we both started crying as we held one another.

Okay, not really. But our conversation *was* a good one. We expressed our frustrations and how the constant pursuit of overwhelmed, overscheduled, and culturally oversaturated teenagers is exhausting. And worst of all, it's turning us into overwhelmed, overscheduled, and culturally oversaturated youth workers.

As we spoke about our frustrations, it felt so good to be known like that, to be understood. We both felt the unique pressure of working in a post-Christian world. Just when you think a spiritual breakthrough has occurred in the life of a student, he or she goes to a party and has oral sex with a complete stranger. This constant back-and-forth, up-and-down, twist-and-turn ministry field is frustrating. And that frustration alone can lead to burnout. But if you pile on top of that a church board or council or maybe even a supervisor who applies constant pressure to grow your numbers, you end up with a stifling work environment. Now throw in a complaining parent who copied your boss into an angry email and *voilà*! I'm not sleeping for the next four days.

Actually, my boss and I did receive an angry email. The writer of the email was being extremely shortsighted, but that doesn't stop me from having a pit in my stomach all day. It's hard to shake those kinds of negative interactions. I know my boss has my back, but sometimes I can begin feeling like I just want to disengage from everything and everyone and move to the Caribbean. That sounds nice. It would be nice to be able to live life without sleepless nights and battles raging in my mind.

But let's leave the world of fantasy and head back to my conversation with my youth pastor friend. He said, "Brock, sometimes I feel like leaving youth ministry and becoming a teaching pastor somewhere. It's like I'm too close, and the job is never done with students. I feel like there's too much pressure to be the perfect youth pastor!" Being in youth ministry now for 23 years, I've had these kinds of thoughts myself. *How much more can I do? Where is God in all of this? Is it okay to euthanize students after they're baptized so they can't backslide?*

Instead of doing something crazy, such as a mass drowning during a baptismal service, I've learned to habitually pursue the heart of God. To run after his peace, his hope, his confidence, and allow him to show me his providential work in the lives of our students. Honestly, though, part of my problem is that I've developed what's called "a messiah complex." In other words, I think it's all up to me and it's all about me. I'm not sure if it's the atmosphere of today's high-pressured churches, my own temperament or, more likely, a combination of the two. But when I'm not on my A-game, this is how the messiah complex plays out in my life: I start believing that the well-being of my students is somehow based upon how I teach, share vision, or run effective programs. I. Me. *I* have to help this complaining mom's son. *I* have to check up on every student and make sure they aren't having sex. If *I* am not out working every night, spending time with students and leaders and parents, then they simply won't make it.

Another name for a messiah complex is Christian narcissism.
It's what happens when ministry is no longer about Jesus and
what he is doing, but it becomes all about me and what I am
doing. When did we turn ministry into an evaluation of worth
based on our ability to keep students on the "straight and
narrow" and our knack for putting butts in the seats? Why do
we take on the additional pressure of keeping families happy
and facilitating amazing student breakthroughs? Count me
out! And you know what? Students are also saying, "Count
me out!" They aren't stupid. They see what's really behind
our event promotions. Big numbers make us feel good and
give us job security. It's not that I think I don't have to work
my butt off. Trust me, I know I do. But am I working hard
while feeling overwhelmed by the reality of God's love and
peace? Or am I just working hard and feeling like I'm failing
at everything?

In that conversation with my fellow youth worker, we began
speaking truth over each other. As this truth started to free us,
we felt lighter, more hopeful, and we were reminded that God
is with us. God is in this with us; he's going to do the work.
He's going to change lives. This is God's heart.

Me? I can't save a soul. I, in my own strength, can't convince
anyone that Jesus' lordship is good, and I definitely can't
change anyone's heart. In 1 Corinthians 1:18-31, the apostle
Paul even said that the gospel message is "foolishness" to
those who don't believe. That means it's going to take the
work of the Holy Spirit to do the convincing. It's not up to
me. Because let's be honest, I can't even change my *own*
heart; I need God to do that. And I needed to be reminded that

God's heart is *for* us. I may be powerless on my own, but God isn't. Every time I give up hope, Jesus shows up. He moves, he saves, and he changes stories. My job? I get to rest in the fact that God loves me and he loves those I minister to. I get to be there to watch him do what he does best. I get to allow him to use me, and I get to be his vessel, his mouthpiece, and his touch. That's my job. I just have to show up with a tender heart.

I think about the culture Jesus was living in. At that time many children were discarded, considered second-class and basically their parents' property. Even the disciples initially had no heart for them. There wasn't a children's pastor or a youth worker on Jesus' team. For the most part, no one was investing in kids, listening to them, or including them. Yet despite this cultural view, Jesus calls the children to himself in Matthew 19:14. *"Jesus said, 'Let the little children come to me, and do not hinder them, for the kingdom of heaven belongs to such as these.'"* I love how Jesus includes them; he even gives them the kingdom. And he says the kingdom is for them now, not just when they're older. This was his heart and his heart hasn't changed. Nothing will prevent Jesus from pursuing the souls of teenagers, not even our manipulative Christian narcissism. He wants them to have his kingdom.

Like the disciples, we are consumed with the norms of our culture. We toil hard for the kingdom and carry the burdens of ministry. But as we're doing those things, we fail to notice the subtle ways Jesus is trying to get our attention throughout the day. If we allowed Jesus to bring peace and rest to our minds, I wonder if we'd be able to see what he is up to?

In fact, here's an assignment: Get outside, go to a park, and just breathe. Do it today. Ask God to give you peace. Ask him to take the blinders off your eyes and remind you of your calling to just be with him.

Isaiah 30:15 is a verse I'd never really noticed until our pastor spoke out of it not long ago, and it totally floored me. It says, *"This is what the Sovereign LORD, the Holy One of Israel, says: 'In repentance and rest is your salvation, in quietness and trust is your strength, but you would have none of it'"* (NIV). That last line sounds like me. I have rejected God's rest for far too long. All I have to do is acknowledge that I am fearfully and wonderfully made. See, we are his creations and we are loved. Our job, our role, is to bask in the love of our Father and remember who is in charge. So if our relationship with God is our true ministry, then basking is a must.

Look at that verse again. It calls us to repent, and I'm beginning to see what I need to repent of. Because by ignoring rest, I am ignoring God's loving presence; by ignoring rest, I am intentionally seeking to break relationship with my Father in heaven. If I go back to the beginning, the seventh day after creation, I am given his instructions on how to be fruitful. This happens by beginning in rest. If I am to be fruitful in the way God has designed me to be, then I have to hear him and know him. How can I possibly do that if I am depleted, shattered, and emotionally run-down? Lastly, by ignoring rest, I am trying to make myself God. I deny that I am a creature, and I pretend that I am the Creator. In truth, I am the beloved steward, not the Master of the universe.

Just a couple of weeks ago, I got a phone call from a former volunteer youth worker who'd become a part-time paid youth worker at a church. I'll say that again: he was *part-time.* Recently he'd been told that he needed to do more in order to keep his job. The lead pastor wanted him to start a student leadership team on top of what he was already doing. Plus, he wanted the youth program to grow numerically. Let me give you a run down on what this part-time youth worker was already doing: a full middle school program, a full high school program, recruiting and training leaders, encouraging and meeting with parents, and on and on. Now he has to add to his to-do list a student leadership program, plus grow the youth group. Any helpful suggestions? Why, yes! Do more events. He told me he's just going to have to work harder to please his boss. He gets paid to work 20 hours per week, but he currently puts in about 50 hours. Do you see what's happening?

As he was talking, I could feel the weight of the world on his shoulders. He was feeling crushed by the pressure to get more students, develop them, rescue them from the strong cultural pull . . . and it still wouldn't be enough. And I'm not sure where his own young family was supposed to fit into the picture. Matthew 11:28 has a word for this youth worker—and for all of us who are burdened by the pressure of working in a ministry that's so demanding. Jesus says, *"Come to me, all of you who are weary and carry heavy burdens, and I will give you rest"* (NLT). God is calling us to rest and to trust in the fact that he has a heart for this new generation. His desires for them will come to pass. I wonder if God is calling us to more rest and less work. I wonder what would happen to our ministries if we began to hear the voice of Jesus again.

But this is a hard line to walk. If I worry over the students in my care, does that mean I'm not trusting God? Life is too complex to be an either/or paradigm. In fact Jesus knew we'd worry. Peter told us to cast all of our anxiety upon Jesus because he cares for us (1 Peter 5:7). And in today's world, there are a hell of a lot of worries that we can cast onto Jesus. Start casting, my friend!

Youth pastors have many sleepless nights, and not just because of junior high lock-ins. It's because by living life with students through the pain of neglect, abuse, mistakes, and the consequences that a post-Christian world produces, I've had to bear the weight of their stories pressing down on me. Many of the details they've shared have tortured me late at night when I'm alone with my thoughts.

One such difficult story began the first time a 13-year-old girl walked into the youth room. By all appearances everything was just fine. She had such energy and a great excitement about her. But behind the façade of laughter and smiles was pain beyond anything you could ever imagine. Something terribly wrong was brewing under the surface.

The girl's grandfather had told me she'd be joining our middle school group, and what brought her to us was rejection in a form that I, personally, struggled to even grasp. Immediately we went to work getting her connected, giving her a mentor, and just making sure we created an environment where she could experience the warmth of God. After about nine months had passed, she came up to me in the church bus and bluntly asked, "Brock, why didn't she pick me?"

About a year prior to her arrival, this girl's mother had taken in a live-in boyfriend. It started well, but inevitably things went downhill. He began picking up the bottle each night; and with each drink, he became more and more angry. As the weeks turned into months, the dysfunction grew, and every night he'd beat the girl's mother. Seeing your mom get beaten on a regular basis by a raging lunatic twice your size must be horrific. The sense of anger, panic, and powerlessness must have been overwhelming. But this little girl was not going to take it, and she began sticking up for her mom, standing in the midst of the abuse. He reacted predictably and started beating her as well.

Eventually some neighbors reported this problem to social services. And a series of events brought her mother before a judge who did not mince words. "This case is simple, lady," the judge said. "You need to pick your daughter or your boyfriend." And so the choice was made.

"Brock, why didn't my mom pick me?" Have you ever been asked a question that you have no clue how to answer? I was at a loss for words. In my mind I prayed a simple prayer, "God, give me something here, PLEASE!"

I paused and then asked the girl a question, "Did you ever ask God—maybe when you were in bed at night and the lights were out and the house was quiet—'God, if you're real, you've got to help me. You have to get me out of this situation.' Did you ever say a prayer like that?"

"Of course I did, many times," she said.

I took a deep breath, "Well, do you think he answered?"

She responded hesitantly and with thoughtfulness, "No, I don't think so. My life is horrible, and I just feel sick inside. But what do you think, Brock?"

I said, "Well, I think he *did* answer you. When you were praying in your room at night and asking him to get you out of that horrible situation, he not only heard you, he answered you. He moved and plucked you out of that place, and he brought you here to us. He heard you all those nights in the dark when you were crying out to him." At this point we were both crying.

And then she whispered, "I never knew. I didn't realize God cared."

God did this! He set the whole thing up. He orchestrated her freedom. He was transforming her life and filling her future with hope. It's true; God is pursuing the hearts of our kids.

This morning I had breakfast with a tenth grade boy. About a year ago, he felt like God was calling him to the military and that somehow, through this, he would be a light to the world. Initially I thought, *Well, that's kind of weird.* But I wisely kept that thought to myself. Shortly after he received this revelation, this student was at a camp in England. He prayed God would give him another picture of what He wanted him to do. Suddenly, a man that he didn't know walked up to him and said that God had given him a picture of the American flag and a ship. This man felt like God was going to use the military, or something like that, as an avenue for this teen boy to be salt and light to the world. He would be a voice of hope to many. When this student got back home he met with me and was overwhelmed with joy that God had answered his prayer.

If you're like me, you kind of doubt this message was actually from God. I mean, surely it's got to be a coincidence! As Sebastian Moore wrote, "In religion, there always lurks the fear that we invented the story of God's love."

God always leaves us that choice. But what I would say from my own experiences is that Jesus just keeps revealing himself to me and to my students who are in way over their heads in a post-Christian world. It just seems like when we are still and silent, when we take the time to open up our lives, God speaks to the deepest strata of our souls.

I asked one of our female students to join me up front during the worship service and share her story with our congregation. She talked about how she struggles to follow Jesus at home, but on mission trips and at camps she experiences him. She said life back home is too busy and too noisy to hear God; but somehow when she takes the time to get away, she finds him.

I said, "Wow, Jen. What you just said reminds me of that verse where Jesus says, *"Ask and it will be given to you; seek and you will find; knock and the door will be opened to you"* (Luke 11:9, NIV).

She looked at me as we stood on that stage, in front of the whole church, and she said into the microphone, "Wow. I never thought of it that way. I never knew that Jesus is always there and that the moment I pick my head up and look for him, I'll find him!" God is pursuing the hearts of our students.

He's even pursuing those who aren't seeking him. He has a heart for the ones who couldn't give a rip about spirituality. Yesterday I was in a meeting with some adults and some students, and we were planning how we might serve the schools in Greenwich and be a blessing to our community. We started talking about how each of us came to faith. One of the teenage guys, who about a year ago was rebellious and completely against Christianity, shared that whenever the topic of religion came up, he'd just rip it apart and belittle anyone who believed in God. But now here he was a year later, sitting in a meeting and talking about how we can be Christ to the schools in our city. Amazing! It reminded me of the story of the apostle Paul, a man who was dead set against the early church and had plans to get rid of this new faith. But God had other plans. He took a young, arrogant zealot and—*ka-pow!*—turned him into a humble servant of Jesus Christ.

In a similar way, God *ka-powed* this young man. It wasn't me, and it wasn't any other leaders who did this. It was all God. In fact, I remember the first time he came to our youth group. As I stepped off the stage after giving the message, I thought, *That was the worst talk I may have ever given. I felt like a failure.* But this kid came up to me and asked to meet with me over coffee. We met a week later, and he told me that while I was speaking, for some reason he'd felt something and it kind of freaked him out. I gave him a book to read, and he devoured it in about two days. Then he called me and said, "Okay, I'm in." This kid has not been the same since. God wanted him. God has a heart for this young man. God is on the move, and he has a vision for our students. But it begins with us resting in and trusting that God's heart is for them.

I am just so grateful and overwhelmed by God's goodness. I am blown away by how he consistently shows up despite my narcissism. God is always working. I've seen this in my own family. I've seen God's heart since I was a little boy. My mom, Carol, is an amazing woman who was raised in a difficult home. From the time she was a little girl, her parents would verbally, physically, and emotionally abuse her. She felt like she never measured up, like she just wasn't good enough.

As a child she had an unusual gifting for music. She was able to play on the piano any tune she heard, and she would frequently make up her own lyrics. As her talents became known, she was regularly asked to accompany singers in church. But her parents made it very clear that they disliked her singing by making fun of her when she sang. The sad irony in all of this is that her name is Carol, which literally means "song." Yet she was mocked for living out her name's meaning.

When she was in her twenties, my mom sang on commercials, television, and was a lead singer for a Christian rock band. Yet at times, her parents treated her as an embarrassment to the family. Abuse is a horrific thing. It skews the way we see others and the way we see ourselves.

The story hits an all-time low, however, when her aged parents invited her to their home. It had been years since they'd even spoken to her, so she went to visit them with high hopes for reconciliation. From the moment she got there, the realization of their true intentions hit her in the face. They began walking her around the house and showing her all of the things she would not inherit when they died. They told her they didn't truly see her as their daughter and she would get nothing. Then they said, "And we don't want you singing at our funerals either."

Have you ever seen someone cry so hard that you actually feel a piece of the pain they're experiencing? It was an overwhelming feeling when my mother came home from that trip broken, hurt, and desperate to hear that she was lovable. My amazing mother, a professional musician and, more importantly, a kind and caring woman, could not get love from her parents.

God knows her pain and the insecurities she carries; and as a good Father, he showed up. Not only did he show up, but he fully redeemed my mom's story. Shortly after she returned home from her trip, Mom was asked to sing and play the piano at the end of the Sunday morning church service. As she quietly sang, a teenager came up to her on the stage and silently sat next to her on the piano bench. It seemed strange, but what happened next is stranger still. This young man whispered these words to my mother, "Carol, I don't know why I'm supposed to tell you this, but God wanted you to know that he loves it when you sing."

God loves it when we sing, when we lead games, when we sit in a coffeehouse with a hurting student and their parents, and when we prepare our messages. He loves it when we pray to him. He loves it when we use our gifts and make people laugh. He wants you to know that not only does he have a heart for your students, but he has a heart for you. He has a plan for you and he is going to use you in remarkable ways. This generation won't be the last Christian generation in America. No way! God has called us to them, and this calling is not in vain. And God has a huge heart for our students. He loves seeing their eyes opened, their hearts softened, and their minds illuminated. It's what he does best. It's his heart. Why do you care so much about these kids that he has given you? Because he has given you his heart for them. He has placed within us his dream and his calling. He's given us his eyes to see students the way he sees them. And we love it when they sing.

Last year I spoke at The Youth Cartel's youth worker event called The Summit. Afterward, I stayed around for the whole event because it was unique and encouraging. One of the presenters was Chris Folmsbee who spoke about hope. He said this, "Most youth workers are leading from a place of despair. They are leading from a place of fear and anxiety because the world they encounter is so full of brokenness and hopelessness. So as I look out at hundreds of youth workers, I hope they join me in a march toward hope. God is in the process of restoring the world to its intended wholeness." And then he said, "See, hope grows in winter."

Many of us look at this broken world, and the spiritual temperature resembles an Alaskan winter. But under the surface, God is working. God is working in the lives of your students in ways you may never know until Jesus' return. But he is working nonetheless, and there is much hope.

But in order to see it, we must remember that it's all about proximity. If I am close to Jesus, I see more. Actually, as I said, my relationship with Jesus *is* my ministry. Everything that Jesus does in me spills over onto those around me. If I'm not spilling, then I'm not ministering.

About a year ago, I'd worked myself into the ground. There had been a long season of working with no days off, and the constant demands of writing, speaking, and ministering at my church were overwhelming me. I got to the point where I felt so dry in my soul, I felt like I was about to crack. I knew what I needed. I needed some R&R and some alone time with Jesus. So I got into my Jeep and headed for the mountains. Deep in the northern part of Connecticut there is a secret swimming hole. No one knows about it except for, like, everyone. But it was the middle of the day. So I parked in the foothills and headed out on a long hike. It was at the end of the winter, and the snow had just melted. The river was running high and fast and loud, and I hiked alongside the roaring water for a couple of miles. I finally stopped at the foot of one of the most beautiful waterfalls you'll ever see. And the mist of the falls was hanging in the air, surrounding me. I stood there and my soul was just soaking it all in.

In that moment I sensed Jesus saying, "Brock, I've got you."

Those words just kept reverberating in my mind and heart. "Brock, I've got you. I've got your students, I've got your ministry, I've got everything! I've got you." I just stood there and made a choice to trust him with everything. I knew that while I slept, he wouldn't. I can't always be there for the students, but he will. When I don't quite measure up, he does. He's got me. So I headed back to my Jeep and drove home.

The next morning we were in prayer as a church staff. Dave, our worship leader, looked at me and said, "Brock, I feel like I have a word from the Lord for you." Normally when people say that, I'm kind of cynical. But this time I was open to it; this was Dave and he is awesome.

"What's the word? I'm ready," I said.

Dave said, "Brock, God is telling you, 'I've got you, you don't need to worry, I've got everything!'"

As we close this book, I feel like you need to know that God is with you, his favor is upon you, and you can trust him. You can rest in the fact that he's got you. God's heart is for you. How great is the love of God? How amazing and detailed and aware is his love for us? What lengths will he go to prove to you that you are treasured, honored, and that your future is amazing? He will go down any path, climb over any obstacle, endure any pain—even the pain of the cross—to express his love for you.

Hear the word of the Lord:
"Do not be afraid, for I have ransomed you;

I have called you by name; you are mine...
You are precious to me. You are honored, and I love you . . .
For the mountains may move and the hills disappear,
but even then my faithful love for you will remain.
My covenant of blessing will never be broken."
— Isaiah 43:1, 4; 54:10 (NLT)

END NOTES

[1] Stuart Murray, *Post-Christendom* (Carlisle, Cumbria: Paternoster, 2004), 19.

[2] Christian Smith, *Soul Searching: The Religious and Spiritual Lives of American Teenagers* (New York: Oxford University Press, 2005).

[3] Albert Mohler, "Transforming Culture: Christian Truth Confronts Post-Christian America," posted July 15, 2004, www.albertmohler.com/2004/07/15/transforming-culture-christian-truth-confronts-post-christian-america/.

[4] "How Post-Christian Is America?" Barna Group, April 15, 2013, www.barna.org/barna-update/culture/608-hpca#.Ue7hExzVps4.

[5] Timothy C. Tennent, *Invitation to World Missions: A Trinitarian Missiology for the Twenty-first Century* (Grand Rapids, MI: Kregel Publications, 2010), 34-37.

[6] Ibid, 35.

[7] Ibid, 35–36.

[8] Ibid, 37.

[9] Robby Butler, "Unlocking Islam: What a Kuwaiti Muslim 'knows' about 'Christianity,'" *The State of the World* (January-February 1991), www.missionfrontiers.org/issue/article/unlocking-islam.

[10] Oswald Chambers, *My Utmost for His Highest* (Grand Rapids, MI: Discovery House Publishers, 1992), 25.

[11] Business Wire, "HealthAmerica KidsHealth Poll Finds Kids Feel Too Busy; 78 Percent of Kids Wish They Had More

Free Time," August 17, 2006, www.businesswire.com/news/ home/20060817005326/en/HealthAmerica-KidsHealth-Poll-Finds-Kids-Feel-Busy.

[12] Taylor Clark, "It's Not the Job Market: The Three Real Reasons Why Americans Are More Anxious Than Ever Before," www.slate.com, posted January 31, 2011, www.slate.com/articles/arts/culturebox/2011/01/its_not_the_job_market.html.

[13] Timothy Smith, *The Seven Cries of Today's Teens: Hearing Their Hearts; Making the Connection* (Brentwood, TN: Integrity Publishers, 2003), 102.

[14] Eugene Peterson, *Working the Angels* (Grand Rapids, MI: Wm. B. Eerdmans Publishing Co., 1987), 2.

[15] American Society of Plastic Surgeons, "Plastic Surgery for Teenagers Briefing Paper," www.plasticsurgery.org/news-and-resources/briefing-papers/plastic-surgery-for-teenagers.html.

[16] American Society for Aesthetic Plastic Surgery (ASAPS), "Teens and Plastic Surgery," Age/Gender Issues, www.surgery.org/media/news-releases/teens-and-plastic-surgery.

[17] Sarah Brooks, "Parents: A Word about Instagram," Life as of Late Blog, posted April 18, 2013, http://taylorandsarah-brooks.blogspot.com/2013/04/parents-word-about-instagram.html.

[18] "Philip Zimbardo: The Demise of Guys?" filmed March 2011 and posted August 2011, www.ted.com/talks/zimchallenge.html.

[19] Focus Adolescent Services, "Alcohol and Teen Drinking," www.focusas.com/Alcohol.html.

[20] C. R. Snyder and Shane J. Lopez, *Positive Psychology* (Thousand Oaks, CA: Sage Publications, Inc., 2007), 260.

[21] Eryn Sun, "America's Got Baggage? Approaching a

Post-Christian World with Tim Keller, Gabe Lyons," posted February 18, 2011, www.christianpost.com/news/americas-got-baggage-approaching-a-post-christian-world-with-tim-keller-gabe-lyons-49042/.

[22] Jim Henderson and Matt Casper, *Jim and Casper Go to Church* (Carol Stream, IL: Tyndale House, 2007), 147.

[23] Kester Brewin, *Signs of Emergence: A Vision for Church That Is Always* (Grand Rapids, MI: Baker Books, 2007), 46.

[24] Donald Miller, *To Own a Dragon* (Colorado Springs: CO, NavPress, 2006), 46–48.